CONQUERING
THE UNDERTOW

LEARNING TO BREATHE AGAIN

SUZANNE RENEE

Conquering the Undertow: Learning to Breathe Again/Renee, Suzanne/Non-Fiction/Self-Help

First paperback edition October 2021

Edited by Writemywrongs, llc

Cover Photo by Mitchell Zachs, MagicalPhotos.com

Cover Design by Germancreative at fiverr.com

Printed in the United States of America for worldwide distribution

Published by Suzanne Renee

Suzannereneeauthor@gmail.com

Suzannerenee.com

Dedicated to those who suffer silently, thinking no one can understand their journey, the ones who struggle to put their experiences into words, the brave souls who feel completely alone yet often hide behind a smile, so no one will know their secret.

TABLE OF CONTENTS

ACKNOWLEDGEMENTS

I'd like to thank my friends, Bonnie, Cebert, Laurie, Caitlin, and Eve for helping me with the initial revising process and sharing much helpful insight.

I'd like to thank my many beta readers, especially my friend Carla, who gave me the confidence to publish this much needed story.

To my friend Stef, thank you for creating a fun space of accountability with me and giving me a reason to get out of bed to write this book.

To my mom, Ray, and younger brother, Rob, thank you for always supporting and loving me no matter what.

To my sister, Jill, thank you for your guidance in both my life and this book's cover.

To my niece, Gabi, thank you for being my light and hope.

To my brother, Richard, and dad, Mel, thank you for showing me the quality of our memories is what really matters.

To my New York friends, thank you for never giving up on me.

To my D.C. and Boston friends, thank you for being part of my journey.

To my Miami friends, for me, you were the magic.

To my first hotel managers, thank you for taking a chance on a girl with little experience but a big dream.

To the amazing Landmark Education souls I encountered, both staff and participants, thank you for sharing yourself so openly with me, so I could grow right along with you.

To my first therapist, Elizabeth, I will never forget the tools you gave me, knowing I could once again have control over my life.

To Tony Robbins, your Comeback Challenge gave me the chance to stop thinking about why I wasn't ready to write this book. You helped me realize I must.

To Brian Mayoral, thank you for creating the step-up community to make sure I didn't forget my *why*.

To my friend, Colton, thank you for seeing my greatness and reminding me that sometimes we create dreams and figure out how to actually make them happen later.

To my friend, Martha, thank you for showing me the simple things in life and that in the end genuine friendship is what really matters.

To my many Facebook communities, thank you for being there for the late nights and times I felt I was alone.

To my cover photographer, Mitchell Zachs (@MagicalPhotos), thank you for your patience as we ran around Miami Beach.

To my website designers, Kozeta and Jonida, thank you for reminding me of my potential.

To Ben and Jade at Tonic Books, thank you for reminding me that writing is not always something we do because we feel like it. Instead, it's a habit that becomes a must if we do it enough.

And to myself, thank you for allowing yourself to feel the good and the bad and to turn the most bitter lemons into lemonade.

PROLOGUE

My name is Suzanne Renee, which means *lily* (Suzanne) *born again* (Renee). Interestingly, it took me thirty-eight years to truly feel born again—to embrace who I really am—and that's exactly what this story is about: rebirth.

There are 365 days in a year. Why do we not celebrate every single one of those days? Why save our gratitude and reflective moments for birthdays, weddings, and anniversaries? Why wait for the big moments to appreciate our lives?

I used to think those blank squares on my calendar, the ones that didn't have a note to remind me of a special event, didn't matter. They were just days to live through, not ones to embrace. They were just another regular, predictable, twenty-four hours.

I placed a lot of importance on planning my next trip or birthday. I forgot every day given to us is special. As time went on, I was getting through the day, yet always feeling something was missing. Often, I was so busy staying occupied with what I thought made me happy that I forgot to stop, pause, and reflect on what actually brought me happiness. Have you ever felt that way?

Those regular normal days ended up being the big ones. I remember days of doubling over in laughter with friends, of staying up late gossiping with my best friend, or baking with my mom. I remember staying out past midnight and feeling like the world was mine.

There were also those mornings when I'd wake up thinking it was another typical day before I'd find out I'd lost my job, a family member, and even my belief in myself. How do we navigate those days we're totally unprepared to handle? Life is a combination of challenging, awful days mixed with breathtaking, exhilarating ones. This only becomes a problem when you're stuck in the perspective that those one or two bad days are your entire life.

I want to take you along on my journey of survival and share the beautiful view I now see every day, one of acceptance and appreciation.

I know what it's like to be in breakdown mode—to wonder if you're cursed or why bad things happen to good people. I, too, have walked around feeling like I'm carrying the weight of the world on my shoulders. The truth is this feeling doesn't go away overnight. I promise, though, that by the end of this book you will walk away with something valuable you can apply to your own life. Perhaps this will move and inspire you to create a different future for yourself.

How often do you reflect on your days and take in the moments and memories? Do you embrace daily how truly lucky you are? I will take you on a journey through my highest highs and lowest lows. I will shift your focus from a feeling of regret to a feeling of celebration. You'll learn about how taking the time to anchor good moments and using those as a reference of hope for the worst days can make a huge difference in coping with the difficult parts of life—not just the big pieces, but the small portions as well.

Now, if you're struggling as I once was, you may not believe me, and you may feel you have nothing to celebrate. If you are grieving from the loss of a parent or still grasping the reality of losing someone to suicide, you may be unsure. If you've experienced suicidal thoughts you may have doubts. If you wake up every day to a toxic job environment or recently lost your job, you may think it will never get better. I get it! I know it seems you'll always be nothing more than a survivor, and the idea of thriving seems impossible.

In this book, you'll meet someone who truly understands your pain, someone who had almost given up but learned how to walk and breathe again, someone who had been through hell yet somehow found a way out of it and is now empowering others to find a way back to the light. I will be that person for you if you let me. I really want this book to make a difference in your life and give you some perspective on what you may be experiencing.

If you're anything like me, maybe you picked up this book because you want to see what it takes to have an amazing life, or maybe you're wondering how someone had the strength to survive so much pain and come out on the other side. Maybe you're feeling stuck, wanting to go to bed the moment you wake up, dragging yourself through life. Perhaps you've experienced trauma or tragedy, and you're trying to make your story one of triumph. Then again, maybe you just want to escape your life for a bit and immerse yourself in someone else's.

Please note this book includes references to topics such as grief, loss, death, suicide, and sexual assault. I share this with you not only so you can better understand me, but to give hope to the many of you brave souls who may have dealt with something similar. I'm honored to share with you some habits and programs that have contributed to my progress, but I cannot guarantee they'll affect everyone in the same way.

These are my stories told from my perspective. I have changed some names to respect the confidentiality of those I talk about. If you picked up this book, you truly care about other people. I know because I am the same way. My goal is that no matter what you've experienced in life, you'll feel more seen and understood and less alone by reading my story.

At the end of each chapter, there will be a reflection, a piece of advice I wish I'd known when these life events occurred in my life. These tips will not magically cure you if you are still processing a challenging life event, but they will arm you with a more powerful toolbox to navigate life. I hope they can be of some value to you on your journey.

CHAPTER 1: WHO ARE YOU?

Our experiences, our education, and our families' values make us who we are today. Yet when we're asked to describe ourselves, we often feel tongue tied. What do I share? Where do I start?

I'm the third of four children. Interestingly, two of my siblings had a different father, my mom's first husband. People would often refer to them as my half siblings, but I'd quickly correct them. Jill and Richard were fourteen and ten when I was born and every bit my brother and sister. There was nothing half or partial about them. My brother, Robert, whom I shared a father with, was four and a half years younger. From the beginning, I struggled to know my place in this hierarchy. Was I the classic middle child always fighting for attention? At times, this was certainly the case. Other times, when my older siblings were out with their friends, I took on the role of the older sister, the responsible, well-behaved child compared to my brother, Rob who always was getting into trouble.

Growing up, I spent a lot of time trying to figure out how to fit in. I always felt I didn't belong. I was different. I realized that no matter what I did, my peers would make fun of me. Part of this occurred because I knew if I raised my hand often, the teachers would like me and give me attention and good grades. The other side of being the teacher's pet is I wasn't as likeable in the other students' eyes. I would walk into the lunchroom with my tray of food and my stomach clenched, take a deep breath, and ask people if I could sit with them. Often, I was told the table was full and a classmate would point me toward another table. Everyone would laugh as I walked away with my head down and shoulders slumped. As we'd all head to class, I'd stay close to my one or two friends, my eyes straight ahead hoping to avoid any more embarrassment. Unfortunately, I'd still hear the other students call out names like "Suzie Scribbles" while pointing and laughing at me. That laughter followed me home, and I continued to hear it as I fell asleep at night. I spent most of my adolescent years being ridiculed.

This only became more difficult in high school where more freedom was allowed. Administrators trusted us to get around, whether it was walking to class or to after school activities. Some of my classmates took this opportunity to break the rules. I would feel peer pressure to join them, but it never felt right to me. One day in sophomore year science class, the teacher, Mr. Collins left the room for a second during a test and someone saw the answer key on his desk and cheated. When he walked back in, I raised my hand and said, "Sir, they took the answers off your desk."

Even though I'd never been taught what to do in situations like this, I had clear views regarding rules and how life should be. I saw the world and every experience as right or wrong, good or bad. There was no gray area. I knew I had to do what was right for me, so that day in class I told the truth, but I quickly learned speaking up for what you believe in can cause isolation, rejection, and shame. When Mr. Collins turned away, I had a bunch of spit balls thrown at my head, and I would bite my lip to keep from crying.

I'll never forget my junior prom when I walked in wearing a long, tight, shiny purple dress. My boyfriend, Walter, was on my arm, and I felt like a million dollars. Immediately, one of the pretty, popular girls (you know, the ones with the perfectly straight blonde hair they never had to battle with a comb) came up to me, smirked, and said, "How much did you pay him?"

I was so shocked I had a hard time making my mouth move enough to have words come out. Finally, after what felt like hours, I remembered how to breathe and mumbled, "Nothing, he's my boyfriend." But by then she'd already flitted away.

I didn't realize it at that moment, but the time I was spending hoping people would approve of me had a tremendous impact on my experience of life. Misfortunes happen, and in those moments, we define our character. Danger arises when we keep fueling this view of ourselves until we believe it to be absolute. In that moment, I decided I wasn't good enough. No matter what I did, people would never like me, and even an experience that should be good, like arriving at a dance with an attractive man would only end in disappointment and pain. I stopped trying to grow, and I chose not to be open to ways I could transform my relationship with myself. Eventually, this attitude became a blind spot—something I trusted was indisputable. I started to tell myself and others, "well that's just how I am." I didn't believe people liked me, and I had a hard time trusting new people didn't have an ulterior motive for being my friend. For a long time, I felt very lost.

Although I was alive, something felt off inside me. I thought I needed to hide behind how others expected me to be.

Transformative Tip #1

How do you decide who you are? Do you accept your identity from comments made by your parents or your peers? Perhaps you interpreted an emotional moment in a certain way, and you used that moment to define your character. Maybe you didn't know the answer in class and believed you were dumb. The more you accept how others define you, the more limited you'll be. If you say, "This is how I am," and you never explore the possibility you're always growing and changing, you'll feel stuck. Allow yourself to be open to the idea that you're a work in progress, learning who you are as you continue to live life. Be open to the idea that you're constantly growing.

How can you explore your identity and the world you live in? Be curious and engaged. We're born with five senses: sight, hearing, smell, taste, and touch. How often do you walk down the street texting people, oblivious to the big, puffy white clouds? What about the feeling of your favorite jeans as you walk, the smell of spring flowers, the taste of your smoothie, or the feeling of your leather purse? I often think about those children's books where you can scratch and sniff, hear sounds, and feel textures. What if we led our lives and were engaged in every moment? What if we were constantly falling in love with life as small children do? Practice incorporating more of your senses in your daily day and catch yourself when you once again become numb to our beautiful world. Too often we have accepted autopilot as life. It's time to say, "No more!"

CHAPTER 2: CELEBRATE YOURSELF

I saw college as a new world, a world where I could truly start over. No one knew who I was in the past. Throughout high school, my one comfort beyond the friends I made from participating in theater was knowing high school wasn't forever. One moment I was a high school freshman, avoiding eye contact in the hallway, and the next I was touring colleges with my mom, seeing what the next chapter could bring. The heaviness in my heart I'd carried for decades from trying to be accepted was unbeknownst to my peers. All I had to do was get accepted into college and then I would no longer have to work on being good enough to meet others' approval. I could just be me.

The summer before college, I attended orientation and immediately fell in love with every element. I stayed up late during those few days talking about everything under the sun. I connected with a nice guy. He was tall and lean with the most beautiful blue eyes. He made me feel so special because he'd chosen to talk to me. My mom had to tell me to stop hugging everyone when she came to pick me up! By the end of that week, after multiple phone calls, Dave became my boyfriend. I was so excited for my new life, filled with great friends and a new relationship to start.

My journal from that time said it best: "When you know what you want, you don't want to wait another day!"

When I went home, the days dragged on. I started a calendar countdown until I began college and was off on an adventure of my own. I loved the idea of meeting people from so many cities, states, and even countries. I no longer had to worry about waking up my mom as I crept up to my room, always landing on the one noisy step that gave me away.

Moving day was my birthday, and I was determined to make it special even though I was away from my friends. Dave gave me three birthday balloons and my new roommate baked me fresh chocolate chip cookies. Walking around in wonder and awe at this campus full of young people like me, I soaked in the special energy that only comes with those first few days of school. I reflected on where I'd been and where I was going. I realized I could be anyone I wanted to be. Any kind of life was now possible. The opportunity to try various clubs, groups, and events and to experience a new perspective was now at my fingertips.

As freshman year began, I wanted to fit in, so I said yes when a girl in my hall invited me to Eclipse, a popular nightclub, and saw a cute guy with jet black hair and a 21+ wristband—a big deal to me in those days. He walked over to me, asked me to dance, and we ended up kissing. I felt so bad afterward I told Dave, even though everyone advised me not to since it was only a kiss.

We tried to work it out, but about a week later, he surprised me by knocking on my door with no notice. I was sitting with a plastic purple bowl filled with microwave mac and cheese while watching a show on my roommates' tiny television. Dave walked in with a dark blue brimmed Yankees hat and his eyes looking down.

I quickly grabbed a hairbrush to fix my hair when he said, "I really like you, but I just can't do this."

My heart broke, and I wiped away my tears as he left the room.

I was such a screwup! The first guy I really cared about and who saw me for who I was had just broken up with me. It was all my fault. I'd hurt him and ruined our chance at something real. Of all the people I met at college, I had known him the longest, and we'd bonded. How could I say goodbye to the guy I immediately connected with at orientation? The guy who had given me hope that my life was finally changing for the better? Maybe that high school girl was right, maybe I wasn't meant to have a boyfriend. I panicked and then scanned the room, hoping to find a way to feel better when my eyes stopped on a bottle of Advil. I grabbed the bottle and shook it as I cried. A few pills came out, and I swallowed them. I kept thinking how mad I was at myself for messing everything up with the one good guy who cared about me. I became a robot, shaking more pills out and swallowing. Shake pill bottle, swallow. Shake pill bottle, swallow. I just wanted to feel better, but I knew I was taking more than recommended. I couldn't stop it. Finally, I gulped for air and knew something was wrong.

I forced myself to stand up. I don't remember consciously choosing my next action. All I knew was I felt this urge to knock on the door of the girl who lived diagonally from me. I had seen her around. She was the one person on the floor who managed to hold a conversation with just about anyone. She had a big smile, seemed really nice, and sent out this energy of comfort, trust, and love. We'd slowly gotten to know each other. I learned she had lived in the county next to the one where I grew up and was getting over a recent breakup as well. For whatever reason, I felt a connection with her. Her name was Christine. The moment she saw me, she knew I wasn't okay. She had such compassion, empathy, and was my calm in the storm. She immediately called to get help, and we forced me to vomit up the medication.

Our friendship may have changed and developed as we've grown older, but we both know we'll always love and care for each other. That moment bonded us for life. When I remember that experience, I think about how even the days we think are super ugly can create a beautiful friendship.

That first college friendship opened up my eyes. Until then, I thought the only point of college was to study and find a job after you graduated. By the end of the four years, my friends had become my family. The first half of freshman year, I spent my time hiding out in my room thinking no one would like me, avoiding eye contact in the hall. After meeting Christine, I realized I'd misjudged the people around me. I slowly started letting people in, and I even smiled at people while walking to class. Although I didn't click with everyone I did make a few close friends on my floor. I quickly learned that I may have been in a new place, but not everyone was meant to be a close friend. The difference was that, unlike high school, there were always new people to meet. I kept attending events and talking to people in class until I finally found my people, the ones who accepted and loved me for who I'd always been. There was no trying, there was just being.

College is a rare experience. There's an expectation at the beginning of adulthood, merely eighteen or nineteen-years-old, to pick a major and know what you're going to do for the rest of your life. All I knew was that I wanted to get good grades, and I enjoyed reading and writing. I picked English as my major. What I was planning to do after college would be another day's dilemma. Initially, I wanted to be a newspaper writer, then a teacher, and then after studying abroad, a travel-writer. I felt like I was just giving people answers to their questions, but I honestly had no idea what I really wanted.

I was the responsible one in my family, the only one of four kids who went away to school for four years. No matter the sacrifice, I needed to be a success story. By my junior year, I realized I needed more direction, so I went to speak with my favorite English teacher from high school, Ms. Kelly. She suggested I look into public relations and maybe a minor in business. I didn't stop to think about what I wanted in a career. When I envisioned my life in five or ten years, where did I see myself? I didn't want to admit I didn't believe in myself, so I looked outward for answers. So, what did I end up doing? That's right—a public relations internship and a minor in business while crossing my fingers and hoping for the best.

As college came to a close, I panicked as I realized it would actually have to end, and I still didn't know what I wanted to do. I was committed to setting myself apart from everyone else and having my whole life figured out by twenty-two. I didn't have time to waste. I had to be perfect.

I attended job fairs and talked to recruiters, but I mostly felt completely overwhelmed. I half-heartedly gave them my resume, knowing I had little interest in most of those jobs. All of this resulted in a significant amount of pressure from within. I constantly worried about the future and was barely sleeping. This became very apparent during my Iceland Sagas class. My current boyfriend, whom I had met during my sophomore year, nicknamed New Dave by my friends, was a computer science major taking the course with me as a fun elective. For me, though, it wasn't fun. It was life or death, and I had to get an A. We both wrote a paper, and when we got it back, I broke down crying and yelling. He got an A, and I got an A *minus*. I know for many an A- is a good grade. But I'd decided I had to be the best. I was the one majoring in English Literature, so how did he outperform me? If I was "Sue, the A minus" as he lovingly called me, then I was nothing.

Isn't it amazing how we focus on feelings centered on what we're not good at rather than all the things we do well? Society teaches us to strive and achieve but not to appreciate the small stuff. Always do more, accomplish more! At least, that was my experience. I was doing so much, yet I was only looking at what I hadn't completed.

Transformative Tip #2

When was the last time you celebrated yourself? Yes, self-celebrate! Why in bookstores do we have a self-help section, but not one for self-celebration? The more you recognize yourself, the more motivated you are. Acknowledge yourself for all that you do rather than looking at the one task you didn't get to finish. Try saying to yourself, "You did a great job today! You woke up and got right out of bed!" Isn't that better than, "What's wrong with you? Why did you miss the train by five minutes? You're a waste." How we speak to ourselves is the most powerful choice we can make to impact our lives.

CHAPTER 3: PLANNING AND FAILING

The day I graduated, May 15, 2004, I couldn't sleep because I kept tossing and turning, thinking about the future. My friends had become my family, and I didn't know how to say goodbye to snuggling in bed, talking until three in the morning, and coming home late after a night out to hear where everyone else went that night. There's so much focus on the grieving process with death, but what about when life chapters end? How does one process the end of friendships or jobs? We're taught not to look back, only to move forward and look ahead. Yet if we don't give ourselves time to grieve and appreciate the life we're leaving, we often leave a part of ourselves in that time period.

When I started my sophomore year, I'd never expected to fall in love. In fact, the day I met my second college boyfriend, coincidentally also named Dave, I barely noticed him. My roommate had known him from the previous year, and while we were all chatting, I mentioned it was my birthday. When he told me it was his, too, I thought he was kidding. That night he accepted my invitation to attend my birthday party and we ended up talking until four in the morning. It turned out having the same birthday wasn't the only thing we had in common, and I especially loved how we each had our "little kid" side. He accepted me for me, flaws and all. I'd often come home to surprise notes or snacks from him, and he was one of the first men in my life I knew I could depend on. No matter how much I'd stress over a test, he always knew exactly how to calm me down and eventually get me to laugh and smile.

We'd been together for three years, and I was starting to think we could work long term. He called me a few days before Thanksgiving of our senior year and asked if he could come over. I happily said "yes" and met him outside my house on the curb.

I ran to him with a big smile, and we shared a quick hug. He then explained he really cared about me but had just gotten a job offer from IBM, and he felt like life was getting too serious. The next logical step for us would have been to move in together. We were only twenty-one, and he wasn't ready for that and thought it best if we broke up. I felt my world implode as I sat on the curb outside after he had driven over to end our three-year relationship. I begrudgingly forced myself to stand up. As I dragged myself into my off-campus house, tears streaming down my face, I realized life was changing. In a few months, everyone I knew and loved would be separated from me across different cities and states.

The pressure to enjoy the present knowing it was fleeting was even more prevalent. As I took lots of pictures and went to senior year rituals, I experienced so many emotions: shock, denial, anger, depression, bargaining, and finally acceptance. I pushed myself into the next phase and tried to date new guys, but my heart wasn't in it. He had been my best friend for three years and while I missed him as my boyfriend, I missed the trust and pure love he gave me even more.

Life after college felt like a slap in the face. After doing everything right, studying, working hard, and taking on extra projects, there was no job in sight. I went to a good school with wonderful friends and didn't get into any trouble. I always thought when you do the right thing, you get rewarded. I really had no idea what to do. A few days after graduation, when all my housemates moved out, I wanted to cross my arms and throw a tantrum. Instead, I took one last look at our off-campus house, left a letter for Christine, who was moving out a few weeks later, and got into my car with the new alumni sticker taped to the back.

I knew college was not the place for me anymore, yet I really didn't want to leave. I'd gained so much and experienced a whole new kind of life full of diversity and spontaneity. Now all of my independence slowly started slipping away. I was going back to my hometown, which I felt I'd outgrown, with no real plan in mind. Once I graduated, I struggled because everything I knew was gone. All I'd taken for granted as part of college life was not the norm in the real world. No more swiping a card with money I didn't earn to make food appear, no waking at 10 a.m. always having a friend to talk to, no wearing pajamas all day. I felt like I didn't belong in this new life.

Every year, the number of people who have a quarter-life crisis between the ages of twenty to thirty is rising. According to Nathan Gehlert, Ph.D., Washington D.C. Psychologist, (How to Power Through Your Quarter-Life Crisis, n.d.) a quarter-life crisis is "a period of intense soul searching and stress occurring in your mid-twenties and early thirties." The typical sufferer is "highly driven and smart but struggling because they feel they're not achieving their potential or feeling they're falling behind." One starts to feel extremely doubtful about their life and choices which is brought on by new found stresses once one enters adulthood. When it happened to me, the term had just surfaced, and my friends laughed when I told them I took books about having a quarter-life crisis out from the library. They assured me I was fine. My brother shook his head and asked if my crisis was about which shoes to wear at night. Loner Wolf.com *(19 Signs You're Experiencing a Quarter Life Crisis (+ Test), 2020)* expands on the quarter life crisis "In this liminal stage of life, where one is neither fully unattached (as in adolescence) nor fully established (as in later adulthood), there can be tremendous psychological and emotional pressure." Overall, you have time on your side regarding your career and physically have a lot more energy. I mean, who is depressed and feeling overwhelmed at twenty-two years of age?

According to the Washington Examiner, *(Millennials struggle with "quarter-life crisis," 2018)* six out of ten people experience a quarter-life crisis. That means 60 percent of each generation is feeling lost for an entire decade, and no one wants to believe it. In time, we forget how hard those years were and say those were the best years of our life. That may be true for some, but for most people, leaving a world of staying up late, partying with lifelong friends just to end up paying student loan debt, commuting for hours, and working a boring nine-to-five job isn't the best compromise. It pains me to see teenagers being told if they work hard and go to college, they can have anything they want.

We're given a blueprint: elementary school, junior high, high school, college, and then what? Unlike generations of the past, we're lucky to have options. As a kid, I loved the *Choose Your Own Adventure* books. Depending on what choice you make, you experience a totally different story. This was fun and entertaining as a book, but when it is my real life, having too many choices resulted in a breakdown and feeling overwhelmed. So how to proceed? Do I pursue more education like an M.B.A.? Should I find an entry-level job? Do I take a gap year and travel? I decided what made the most sense was to move home for a few months, spend time with my family (especially my one-year-old niece), and avoid facing reality.

Transformative Tip #3

When you hear the word *plan,* what do you think about? Does stress, work, responsibility, and maybe, discipline come to mind? Planning can be scary. If we don't deliver on the plan, we fear disappointment. What can be truly upsetting, however, is spending years dreaming about the life you want and never experiencing it. You will most likely fail many times before you succeed. A plan is a way of checking in on your progress. Write your action steps and when you wish to complete each step. Pick a way, and if that way isn't right for you, pick another way to achieve your goals or create a new dream entirely. Failure can be an amazing gift. Failing is a chance to reflect on what worked and what didn't work before planning again. Stop blaming yourself for not getting it perfect the first time. It will make your next try more successful once you apply what you learned the time before. YOU are not a failure. Don't judge yourself as wrong or bad. Instead, view failure as an opportunity to reflect on what happened.

CHAPTER 4: NO DECISION IS PERMANENT

The summer after college, I moved home to find not much had changed. I'd graduated with honors, but after many job fairs and interviews, I still couldn't land something full time. It was almost like being in a time warp. I'd just accomplished what I'd spent my entire life working for: a bachelor's. I was supposed to be living in some big city with a high paying job! My life was destined to be an episode of *Friends* or *Sex and the City*—not *Gilmore Girls*.

My mom would tell me the garbage can was my friend, and I should throw all my college memorabilia out. I knew I had to start my post college chapter but wasn't yet ready to accept I wouldn't be going back. She tried to make me feel at home, even making my favorite dinner, but being in that house no longer felt like a place where I belonged.

My childhood home didn't feel like it was the same place I'd left just four short years ago. I'd met people from all around the world and learned how to depend on myself. I wasn't sure how to navigate being back home, and in many ways, it felt like I was regressing. Growing up, I loved to spend time in my room with the posters from shows I was in and the bookshelf full of books. Now all I wanted was to be back in my off-campus house or even a college dorm. I was no longer a student, yet I wasn't working, so I wasn't sure what to do with myself.

Thanks to a good friend, I eventually took a summer job as an arts center receptionist and camp registrar. There were only five people in the entire office. While they were kind, flexible, and lovely, there were very few opportunities for growth. Originally, I was hired to help with the busy camp and classes during summer. They knew this was not my forever job but were happy to have me help them for a few months. My goal was to find a full-time position in public relations starting in the fall. They allowed me to take repeated days off to travel the forty-five-minute bumpy bus ride to New York City to interview once a week. However, nothing was working out.

Summer turned into fall, fall turned into winter, and after each interview, I kept asking myself, "Do I really want a job like this?" The idea of working a job that was so much about reaching financial goals and making commissions didn't evoke my passion. The answer to my question was clearly a "no" in my gut and heart. The pressure I felt when I thought about working in a Manhattan public relations firm was unsettling. At least that was the energy and impression I got from the interviews. I didn't want to let my family down, though. They always expected me to be the golden child and a high achiever. So, I kept applying because I was living for other people and not for myself.

Besides the job search pressure, my house had gotten very crowded. Somehow all my siblings were back home, too! They were all a little older, but still fighting and bonding under one roof.

My sister, Jill, after living in both New York City and Miami Beach, was a single mom with an infant who moved back to get support from the family. She'd work at night and be busy with my niece during the day. My older brother, Richard, who'd lived in California and Florida, would close his door, strum his guitar and sing soulful songs with his heartfelt voice. My niece, Gabi, would push the door open, crawl into his room, and my brother would yell at me to come get her. My younger brother, Rob, would be outside skateboarding and playing with his friends.

But where was I? I was nowhere. At least that's what I told myself and how I felt. I had just come off the college high. Most of my high school friends had moved to exciting big cities after they graduated from college. Being "nowhere" after all these years of hard work had me feeling small and disappointed in myself.

After a while, I stopped striving for those jobs in Manhattan. I was tired of commuting just to receive a rejection email. I was done with getting my hopes up. I went through the motions thinking I had to figure something out, some way to stop feeling stuck in this boring, small-town life. Growth is huge to us as individuals in order to feel motivated in life. While many people surrounded me, I still felt very much alone. I was determined this was not where my story would end. I wasn't meant to spend the rest of my life in this town and in my childhood bedroom. I kept thinking of that line in the song from *Beauty and the Beast* (*Menken & Ashman, 1991*) "I want adventure in the great wide somewhere, I want it more than I can tell."

I came home one summer's day from the beach with friends, and I don't know what happened, but my soul took flight. After a great day at the Jersey Shore, I wanted to stay listening to the waves. I was ready for my next adventure! At that moment, it became clear. I didn't know how it would happen, but I had to get out of there.

In my gut, I knew the answer. Take action! Move somewhere new. Not just think and dream about a different life, but actually make it happen.

I came home and put a plan in place. I announced to my mom, "I'm moving to Miami."

Around this time, Kelly Clarkson's "Breakaway" *(Clarkson, 2004)* was released. So much of the song resonated with me. Even today when I hear it, I sing it at the top of my lungs: "Out of the darkness and into the sun, I won't forget all the ones that I love. I'll take a risk, take a chance, make a change, and break away!"

This song made me realize I'd wasted too much time thinking about all the options available to me. It was time to pick one and go with it! What's important in life is realizing no decision is permanent. We often spend so much time in our heads analyzing our choices instead of just making a decision and dealing with the consequences after.

My older sister and brother had lived in Miami before, and it was the answer to my lack of a job, my emptiness over losing my first love, and my living at home. Miami Beach, Florida, was the only place I could think of that would be the total opposite of my small upstate, northeastern town.

I have to share that my time in transition in my New York City suburb wasn't all bad. The universe showed me two very important things. First, the temporary job at the arts center introduced me to one of my passions—taking care of people. I enjoyed being their resource, solving their problems, and creating memories. This led me to hospitality, the area I fell in love with, and what would be my driving force in my plan to move to Florida! Instead of investing my time and energy traveling to the city for job interviews in an industry I wasn't really passionate about, I'd move somewhere where hospitality was the major industry.

Second, my eighteen-month-old niece, Gabi, taught me a lesson. She showed me what true love and acceptance were. Little kids are amazing, and we embrace them for who they are, no questions asked. There is no judgment because they don't work according to schedule. Sometimes they wake you up at three in the morning or throw a toy at your head, yet we still love them and don't hold that one moment as defining who they are. We celebrate every small milestone they accomplish. As adults, we love and accept kids and receive the same back in return. Maybe if we were a little kinder to ourselves, we'd receive that kindness back as well.

I hesitated leaving my niece, but my sister said, "You will have your own one day. Go take care of you."

This was the best gift someone could've given me. After spending so many years living for others, the permission to put myself first was exhilarating! That summer day would prove to be a turning point.

My mom was completely shocked by my decision, but she knew I was an adult at this point, and she couldn't stop me. My older brother and sister, Richard and Jill, advised me not to go. They said it wasn't the place for me, and bad things happened there. Still, I was determined to prove them wrong. I knew Miami would work out.

By January, this desire had become a necessity, one that would keep me up at night. As Naranyana Murthy stated (*Nothing is as painful as staying stuck - Narayana Murthy*, 2021) "Growth is painful. Change is painful. But, nothing is as painful as staying stuck where you do not belong." On January 26, 2005, I took two suitcases and moved to my dad's house in South Florida until I could afford a place of my own.

Transformative Tip #4

No decision is permanent. We often spend so much time in our heads analyzing our choices, instead of just making one and dealing with the consequences after. If you accept a job you don't love, you can quit and find a new one! If you move to a city that isn't the right fit, you can move. You can always reassess, and create a new path.

CHAPTER 5: BE INTENTIONAL

The moment I got off the plane in West Palm Beach, I knew life would never be the same. I loved the smiles on everyone's faces, the relaxed energy, and that I was in shorts in January! Even the humidity felt like a warm hug as I exited the plane. I could already see the ocean in my mind. The beautiful environment coupled with actually accomplishing one of my goals was indescribable. I had such an immense sense of pride in having made a dream into a reality. I learned the power that came with having a strong, clear vision that nothing could shake. This mentality differs from wanting, wishing, or hoping. It's knowing without a doubt that you will have the future you want to create. I pictured my life in my mind, but this time it was a glamorous one. The vision I created was a beautiful oceanfront hotel, surrounded by palm trees, and I saw myself at the front desk greeting people as soon as they walked in.

So off I went, determined to put my failed past behind me—the kids who were mean when they barely knew me, the heartbreaks, the lack of job opportunities. When I got to my dad's house, I borrowed his yellow corvette and slowly cruised down Interstate 95, passing Boca and Fort Lauderdale before finally getting to the Miami Beach art deco welcome sign. I felt like my life was finally starting!

In 2005, hotels didn't post open jobs on the internet. You needed to go in person to submit a paper application. I would go door to door, hotel to hotel, with my resume. I was committed to getting a job at an oceanfront hotel. I could see it in my mind as if it had already happened. Day after day, I'd drive back to my dad's house with no job offers. Each day it would become harder to leave Miami. There was just something in the Latin/Caribbean energy that kept whispering, "Don't go, stay here."

I'd drive home, thinking I was a college graduate, so everyone would want to hire me for an entry-level job. Sadly, I was mistaken. Most of the hotels wanted people who'd worked in hospitality before or who knew the area well. Yet I chose to not get discouraged, as I knew I would get what I wanted. I knew it might take some time, but someone was going to hire me. I had learned to finally believe in myself and my dreams.

Two weeks after my search began, after another long day of interviewing, I was sitting on the beach being lulled to sleep by the waves of the ocean dreading my long drive home. Ring, ring, ring! I jumped up and tried to walk to a less crowded area.

The woman on the phone said, "Sue, this is Millie from the Ocean Beach Resort and Spa. We would like to offer you a front desk agent position. Your first day will be February twenty-eighth."

I couldn't stop smiling, and as I walked, it felt like I was floating. With those words, life in Miami was no longer a dream or fantasy. It had just become a real possibility.

The job offer was exciting, but it was bigger than that. I realized my good grades and experience didn't matter. What made the difference, what made them hire me, was my passion for hospitality. My desire to brighten another person's day. I would be true to myself and not be ashamed to let myself be seen. That moment was the first time I understood why Miami was called the "Magic City." There, a twenty-one-year-old girl with no hospitality or big city experience could have her dreams come true. I could leave that nerdy, disliked, unpopular girl behind and be anyone I wanted.

I drove home, windows open with my car radio celebrating with me, playing, "Welcome to Miami, Bienvenidos a Miami." (Smith, 1998) (Thank you, Will Smith!) I was elated, yet part of me still felt as if it weren't real. I landed a job as a front desk agent at a historical oceanfront hotel in Miami Beach! I returned to my dad's house and immediately started packing. Although I had nowhere to stay, I told him I was moving to Miami the next day. I realized I had the chance to become anyone I wanted to be. No one knew me or my history. I was not my past; I was only my future.

I wish I could say my story ended here, and the rest of my days were filled with only beaches and mojitos, but that was not the case.

First, I needed to find an apartment. Luckily, I was able to stay with my sister's friend, Jenny, until I found one. She lived in a studio apartment, and I had to share her air mattress, but I was so committed to my dream that it didn't matter. Jenny and her friends would stay up all hours of the night, but I told myself I was only a guest and would find my own place soon. I was only making eight dollars an hour, so I had a hard time finding an apartment that wasn't infested with cockroaches or termites. I was new to the area, so I reached out to a real estate agent to view some apartments.

My dad offered to come down and help me choose. At twenty-one, I was overwhelmed by the idea of finding my own place, and as much as I wanted to be independent and grown up, I accepted his offer. After a few misses, the realtor took my dad and I to a building right in the middle of South Beach, and while I didn't love the train car style, where the rooms are in one long line after each other as opposed to a central living room and all the other rooms feeding off it, I loved the fact that it was being renovated with all new appliances and paint. The apartment was out of my budget, but my dad offered to help, so I put my pride aside and allowed him to contribute. The realtor told me the apartment would be ready in a few weeks, so I signed on the dotted line. I finally had a place of my own. I dreamed of the day I could invite my college friends, like Christine, down to visit. I would show them my new paradise and how proud they would be that I had created this new existence.

Two weeks later this pride turned into annoyance as I would creep over and peer in the window to see the progress and saw no one was working on my apartment! When I asked the realtor what was going on, he said this was Miami, and that the workers often took half days to go to the beach. I realized at that moment that I would need to adjust to the Miami Beach culture. It was one where people only worked half a day and arriving ten to fifteen minutes late was the norm. I should've been happy I had signed a lease to live there, but the lack of urgency made me feel hopeless. I kept telling myself it was worth it for my long-term dream, but as weeks turned into months, I felt frustrated. One night, while staying with Jenny, it all hit me. I was thousands of miles away from everyone and everything I knew, and I didn't know when I would have my own home. I'd moved down with no real plan, and I couldn't even ask a friend to come meet me as I had no friends in the area. Her studio felt tiny, and while I appreciated her hospitality, I had to get out of there!

While I didn't have anywhere to go, I knew it had been too many days in someone else's tiny space. I just wanted some quiet and a place of my own. My gut said just leave and figure out a new solution tomorrow. I got up and left with my stuff in the middle of the night! I didn't know where to go, so I drove to my work parking lot, parked the car, and laid down in the back seat to fall asleep. I wouldn't even call it sleep because I kept jolting awake every few hours, fearing the police would find me and ask why I was sleeping in my car. I showered at the hotel's staff area. No one needed to know my situation. As the second night began, I was really worried and scared, so I called my older brother, Richard, and told him what was going on. He immediately called around to his old friends, and by the next night, I had a new place to stay. His two friends told me to meet them at the hotel they worked at. They were kind and quiet, and under normal circumstances, people I would've tried to become friends with. Yet, staying with people I had never met before made me feel guilty for bothering them. The house was only one level and was overall very compact. The couch I slept on took up the entire living room area. I spent my time feeling like an obligation rather than a houseguest, and I wished I could give them a definite answer for how long I would be staying. I didn't want to once again overstay my welcome. After I lived there for a few weeks, I purchased them a bottle of wine as a thank you and called my realtor.

My realtor said he knew a hotel they could put me up in, and I was all excited until I got there. It was the most basic hotel I'd ever seen—more of a motel. The building was decaying and smelled of mildew. When I came home every night, I'd hear moaning sounds and soon realized prostitutes surrounded me. After staying just a few nights, I stood up for myself. I told him I needed another solution and that I didn't feel safe there. The next day, he called and said his friend was renovating a two-bedroom apartment in a luxury building with parking nearby, so I quickly accepted.

I moved in only to realize the nightmare would continue! In the bathroom, the shower door was totally off its hinges. Not to mention the contractors would arrive at 7 a.m. each day to do their work. It wasn't a great scenario, but it was an upscale building and was safe and quiet. Since I wasn't going to buy any furniture until I actually moved, I was sleeping on the floor with a blanket and pillows I made into a makeshift mattress. Next to my "bed" was my class of 2004 photo frame with myself, Christine, and two of our other housemates, May and Ling, at graduation. Their faces kept me going. Finally, May 5th came, and my apartment was ready, and not a day too soon.

It's remarkable how when you finally get what you want, it rarely lives up to the picture you had built in your head. As I finished moving in, a Jack Russell dog ran in, and I looked up to see my new neighbor, who ended up being Jenny. Unexpectedly, she had moved next door. She'd play loud music all night, and Dillon, her dog, would run into my apartment day and night trying to eat my stuffed animals. I wondered what I'd gotten myself into. This wasn't college, where friends were just waiting on your doorstep. I would need to create a social group again. When I was at the beach, I would scroll through my phone and realize I was all alone. I'd made a few friends at work, but it was often hard to coordinate seeing each other. The hotel never closed, so someone always had to be there. Our schedules and shifts changed weekly, so planning in advance was nearly impossible.

One evening, I was invited to a party. I was so ecstatic to attend my first South Beach party that I spent hours on my hair and makeup and rushed out the door feeling an electric energy in the air. Shortly after arriving for the gathering, I was looking out the fifth-floor window of the apartment when I was approached by a gentleman.

We began talking, and then he asked, "So what building do you own downtown?"

He continued to talk to me, but I realized I had nothing to say to this group of people. I didn't belong there. At that moment, I knew as hard as I was trying to be one of them, I was completely out of my element. I felt uncomfortable, like I was pretending to be someone else. I ran out of the party crying. I wasn't rich; I wasn't glamorous; I wasn't a celebrity. What was I doing there? Once again, I wiped my tears, and—you guessed it—they just kept coming.

I went home that night and Googled how to meet people in Miami. I thought nothing would come from the internet search, so I could find a reason to let myself off the hook and move back home. I was shocked when a website popped up, which turned out to be the answer to my prayers. Meetin.org was similar to what is now Meetup.com except instead of having specific focuses, the group was created to meet people from all different kinds of backgrounds and interests. Many were new to the area or had moved away and had moved back recently. Today, meetups are everywhere and are accepted as a simple way for people to connect. For me though, it was mind blowing. I asked this machine to find me friends, and bam! Friends!

By 2005, the world was just realizing what an amazing invention the internet was and how it could make our lives even better. I definitely thought it was magical because one day I was sad and lonely with no friends, and the next, I was out in the Miami nightlife with strangers who felt like family. My first birthday in a new city was anything but sad and lonely. Although I'd only been to one Meetin.org event, I posted a birthday celebration for myself on the website. I fully expected maybe one or two people to show up, especially since it was during Hurricane Katrina, but as luck would have it, twenty-five people showed! They were the most amazing, genuine, authentic, and accepting people. They truly cared about who I was as a person and not the building I owned or the money I made. Maybe if I had these people in my life, I could make it here. My birthday wish that year, and for many years after, was to have more time with these new friends building unforgettable memories. Maybe Miami could be my future after all. It was a miracle!

The next set of months passed in a happy blur, and I was able to completely be myself. When the main organizer of the Miami Chapter of Meetin.org stepped down, I took over leading. I walked around with my head held high feeling like a celebrity. Everywhere I went, people would run up to me and ask, "Are you Sue?" I was given complete authority to plan events for the group. I would pick places I assumed I would have no choice but to go to alone, and every single time a record number of people would show up to the event.

One day, I woke up and realized I'd created the life of my dreams. I wasn't that unpopular sixteen-year-old girl at junior prom. Instead, I was well liked and ran all the social events. I ruled that magic city, Miami, where men who looked like models would stride across the room to talk to me. Free drinks were around every corner, and the whole world loved me. I was never so proud to have recreated myself. I gained the confidence I'd very much been lacking, and with that pride in myself, I was equipped to make an even bigger difference for others.

As the years went on, people in the group would grow, move on with their lives, and get married, yet miraculously the bonds made during those late, crazy, unpredictable nights provided me with some of my best friends. Their ability to be completely open, to never judge me or my choices, made me fall completely in love with the kind of people they were. I felt that I belonged. I had found people just like me in a city that was a completely different world than any I had experienced.

My weeks consisted of working the evening shift, typically 3 p.m. to 12 a.m., then meeting my friends at the club and dancing until 6 a.m. and watching the sun come up. "Work hard, play hard" became my mentality. My life became about dedicating myself to taking care of others. In my professional life, I'd become well known at the front desk by our repeat guests who would ask for me by name on my days off. In my personal life, I helped other young professionals, who in their twenties and thirties, realized they had to find new ways of making friends. I loved being an organizer of Meetin.org. It was my own way of giving back to an organization that had given me so much. Living in Miami meant constant visitors, and my calendar quickly filled up with visits from my New York friends. I would show them around Miami, now my city, with pride. To make this place feel more permanent, I decided to adopt a pet. I wanted a pet that could keep me company but allow me to be young and free traveling as I pleased. I walked around the pet store eventually settling on two turtles named Mini T and Rascal. No matter how late I came home, they would swim like crazy as soon as I opened the door, making me feel loved and less lonely.

When my now three-year-old niece visited, she would call the city MY-ami, and I'd smile as it truly had become my home, my place, and my dream come true. I would come home from work with the biggest smile on my face. Connecting with the guests, surprising them, and exceeding their expectations made me realize how lucky I was to be paid for what I did. However, my parents weren't so pleased with my decision.

My mom would comment, "I spent all that money for your college for you to make people keys for a living? Do something else so you can make more money. After all, a job is just a job."

It's hard when it comes to different generations' perceptions. I was taught to value different things than she was. The concept of a job being something one enjoyed was as foreign to her as working in the same position in the same company for forty years was to me. Hearing these comments put a rain on my parade, though. Without her knowing, the impact went straight to my heart.

In September, a sales manager approached me to work for him. I'd just spent my first six months at the front desk with one goal in mind, which was to have fun and to make people leave lighter than they were when they came in. I aimed to just be happy and feel good. Some may say I should've had a plan or a list of goals, but just enjoying what I did worked for me. Hospitality felt effortless. I would have gladly gone to work every day even if I wasn't paid. I knew hospitality wasn't just something to pay the rent; it was my passion. I was promoted to sales and acknowledged as September's employee of the month at the same time.

Moving to sales was highly desired by many front desk employees but I began to regret my decision. Being stuck behind a desk all day, not seeing people's faces, and only talking to them on the phone felt boring. Often, I would stop by the front desk to ask a question, and feel so excited that the next thing I knew, I was behind the desk helping to check people in. Every day, my boss would say, "Thanks for today," which some may think was nice, but to me, it felt like I was in Groundhog's Day. He never told me what specifically he appreciated. It felt like a "thanks for showing up." On the other hand, having a sales job gave me a predictable schedule, working 10 a.m. to 6 p.m. from Monday to Friday. My social life was incredible as I got to know more people and began to not only organize but be invited to many events and happenings.

As time went on, I knew I had a hard decision to make. Do I stay in sales even if my heart isn't in it and embrace my social life outside of work, or do I go back to the front desk and sacrifice my time with my friends?

I spoke to my manager, and she really made a difference. If she was selfish, she would have persuaded me to stay in sales, so she wouldn't have to replace me. Turns out, she really wanted the best for me and came up with the idea for me to do sales five days a week and the front desk one day a week. After a few weeks, I realized my soul craved that one day a week. I would wake up and run out the door to get to work. Still, when I'd share with people I was in sales, I'd get a response of awe and respect. When I told people I worked at the front desk, it would be a much more tempered response.

I had a hard time deciding what to do because by going back to the front desk, I felt like I was letting my family down. My parents would tell people, "Oh my daughter? Yes, she's in sales." They said it as if this was some big, important thing. To them, a sales job was more bragworthy than just being behind the front desk. Little did they know, working at the front desk was a lot more challenging than it appeared. I had to learn how to deal with all different types of personalities and how to turn around guests who were really disappointed with their experience. My mind raced, and I had trouble sleeping at night. I knew my choice was important and would have an impact on my career that could last the rest of my life.

So, what did I do? I went to my comfort place. The one place I knew I could always count on: the library. This was where I discovered the idea of a quarter-life crisis. I took out six books, hoping they would help me with my decision. Instead, I only felt more overwhelmed. While our parents may not have had enough choices, we have too many. Where to live? What career to have? Who to date? How much to save? To buy or rent? What do I want out of life? Where do I want to be in ten years? Should I go back to school? Stay with the same company or apply outward? We grew up with parents who worked hard, stayed with the same company for their entire career, often only had one career path, and often stayed in the same city or state they grew up in. I asked my parents for advice, but they just didn't understand.

I talked to my bosses and coworkers yet didn't feel any better. I spoke to my friends and read books, which didn't help much. No one seemed to have the answer. I still felt anxious and unconfident. I knew I wasn't the only one experiencing this sense of insecurity and doubt. Yet, I felt alone. I put overwhelming pressure on myself to make the right decisions. What if I failed? What if I let down everyone who cares about me? What if I mess up this thing called adulting?

Why do we fear taking risks so much? What if we changed the mentality around failure? It should be celebrated because it means we tried. What if we accept that nothing in life is guaranteed to be permanent: not a company, not a city, not a relationship? What would it be like if the person who lost the race celebrated the fact they were able to finish? They didn't just quit and give up. Yes, we should look at how to improve. Yes, we should expect greatness from ourselves. But we also need kindness; we also need forgiveness and gentleness. We need to feel as if mistakes are okay, so we can learn. I always think about that classic scene in movies and TV when the big red F on a paper is shown, and the character physically sinks lower into his or her chair. Imagine how that person grows up and goes into life. Why even bother if you've already decided you're a failure?

A quarter-life crisis is a serious thing, often leading to depression, anxiety, and even suicide. Yet most people respond as if the person suffering is making too big a deal out of life. The world doesn't want to see stressed, confused young adults. Older people I'd talk to would tell me, "You're young, have fun!" or "You're lucky, I never had this many options when I was your age!"

Instead of spending time getting to know myself, I would compare my life to everyone I was "friends" with on social media. Every time I made a choice, I would look toward others to check if my decision was the right one. Theodore Roosevelt (20 Brilliant Theodore Roosevelt Quotes on Leadership and Life, 2019) declared, "Comparison is the thief of joy," and I have never heard a truer statement. No matter the experience, no matter the choice, I would wonder where I was compared to other people my age. I constantly saw life as a race, one where no matter how hard I tried I could never keep up. A question arose: Was this a marathon I could win, or would I burn out from exhaustion?

Staying up late scrolling through social media only created debilitating thoughts of what a good life looked like. For many, accessing the internet zone causes you to completely lose track of time. It can also result in a lack of sleep and depression. I would come home from work at 1 a.m. and log on to socialize. Before the days of social media, I would have curled up with a good book, but now I could chat the night away talking to people or wonder about what happened to my high school crush and search until I found him. Most of my friends were already in bed since they worked from 9 a.m. to 5 p.m., and I always felt I was missing out on their happy hour because it was in person hours before. I would make myself a drink and stay online for two to three hours talking to a few night owl friends and scrolling through large amounts of status updates and pictures of acquaintances. Many I barely knew or hadn't talked to in years, yet I cared about what they were doing and what they had accomplished. I never questioned what was being posted, I just assumed it was the truth.

Transformative Tip #5

How many hours a day do you spend on social media rather than being present in the world? Is it truly contributing to your life?

Be intentional with your usage of social media. Many of us were introduced to social media and never questioned if it was truly supporting our happiness. Limit your time scrolling the internet. You really can't judge a book by its cover. Once I accepted that most people online are posting their best life, weeding out the pictures where they look tired or angry, I finally gained some peace. It makes people feel better to create this fantasy life and convince viewers of how great everything is going. Their followers are left unsettled, wondering what it would be like to have everything in their own lives be perfect. The truth is we'll never know because there is no such thing as a perfect life, and editing, or using filters, is not a true representation.

CHAPTER 6: LIVE TO MAKE YOU PROUD

Remember those breathtaking days I mentioned earlier? By January 2007, I felt a shift. The various components of my life were falling into place. I'd been in Miami for two years, and I knew the best places to eat and the nicest area of the beach. I was no longer new to the field of hospitality, and I thought about management opportunities. I could finally celebrate my journey, and all I'd accomplished on my own. New apartment, new job, new friends: I could have it all!

One Saturday night, I hosted a Meetin.org event at a hotel's rooftop bar. My group was basically the only people there, beyond a few couples holding hands. I slowly looked around, breathed it in, and then my dad called. I looked at the phone and expressed annoyance. Why did he always call when I was in the middle of something? What did he need?

Growing up, I looked up to my dad. He had this big Santa Claus belly, and my heart would fill just by being with him. I'd make him laugh so much his stomach would jiggle. I remember he let me walk up his legs one foot at a time. I'd start to wobble, and he'd grip my hands and wrists and then flip me upside down. I wasn't scared because I knew he had me.

Unfortunately, when it came to my parents' marriage, I did worry and fear. There was more fighting and tears than laughter. My dad's coping mechanism was similar in some ways to mine. He would smile and laugh in public like nothing was bothering him. What made it different, though, was how he would physically hide himself and use the computer and chat rooms to avoid dealing with the reality of his feelings and his marriage.

I'll never forget coming home from school at twelve-years-old only to find him in the basement with a locked door. I wanted to knock and talk to him, but I heard him intimately conversing with a woman on the internet, and I didn't want to interrupt. That closed door would affect the relationship I had with my dad as well as the relationship I had with myself for the rest of my life. It's amazing how we can make one snapshot of our lives take on so much meaning. I decided I wasn't important to him, that people didn't want to let me in, and that my dad would never love me as much as he loved those women. I went up to my room and cried. As the years went on and the fighting got worse, I pulled away from him.

When I moved in with him after landing in Florida, I didn't want to stay long, and therefore drove to Miami to get a job right away. There was a big gap between us, and my heart was hard and closed off no matter how much he tried. He would do so much for others, but never took care of himself. I walked into his house filled with cigarette butts, unhealthy food, and the smell of smoke and musk. I vowed I would never be like him. When he would visit, I'd walk three feet in front of him because I was ashamed and still hurting. I never told him about that day after school.

I sometimes thought about cutting off communication with him. After so many years and hours of being unable to sleep, he'd turned into a shadow of the father I remembered from childhood. Yet, I felt an obligation and, underneath it all, a feeling of guilt for loving him so much and not being able to tell him. That January night, he left me a voicemail. He said he loved me and would talk to me tomorrow.

The next day, as I was happily walking home from brunch, my mom called me. I debated whether to answer but finally picked up. "I have to tell you something," she shared in a voice I had never heard before. She was rambling, and I had to slow her down.

"Rob was supposed to meet your dad for lunch today. He didn't answer his phone after a few hours, and we became concerned."

Even though I was afraid to hear the answer, my voice wobbled as I asked, "Is he okay?"

She replied, "No. We called the police. I'm so sorry, Sue. They found him on the bathroom floor. He had a heart attack. He died."

The world swirled around me, and I felt like I might pass out.

I yelled at the sky, "Why, God, why? Why? Why?"

I had trouble standing, but I managed to make it another block to my house. I could barely get the key to open the door. Once inside, I crumpled to the floor, unable to believe her. I was only just out of college. How could this happen? How could I live without him?

My dad, who would stay on the phone with me at 2 a.m. to help me parallel park my car after work, was found not breathing, alone on the bathroom floor.

My friends tried to be there for me, but I was twenty-four, and they couldn't really understand. I couldn't explain the gut-wrenching pain and rush of emotions that happen when you realize all the future stories you will never be able to tell that person. I knew we'd grown apart, but I always believed at some point we'd be close again. One day, we would heal the conflict between us, and I would finally be able to reach him. Now that day would never happen. I hated feeling different than everyone I knew. The weight of what happened and how my life would never be the same again was just too much to bear. I had waited too long. He was gone. He wouldn't be at my wedding. He wouldn't meet my kids one day. He just wasn't alive anymore.

I often asked myself if it would've been easier if he'd had a long-term disease, and we knew his time was coming for months or years. As time went on, I realized loss, especially of a parent, is never easy whether closure is available or not. We assume they will always be only a phone call away until one day we must be the grown-ups and learn to exist without them. My mentality transitioned from one of just keeping it together to one of needing to make something of this pain. I decided the way to cope was to make him proud. My need to be perfect and accomplished catapulted. I no longer focused on filling my need for socialization and connection. I no longer felt light and free; I only felt anger and determination.

For some reason, the conversation that kept replaying itself in my head was one we had shared the last time he visited. We were speaking about work when he asked me, "Sue, when are you going to be a general manager already?"

I started not being able to sleep, thinking about how short life was and how I was behind. I was letting my dad down because I wasn't in a leadership position.

At that point, the hotel announced they were closing for a complete renovation. All I could feel was sad. As much as having variety in our lives is important, so is the feeling of stability and consistency. My feelings of insecurity over my choices were only exacerbated. The one constant I had known since I had moved to Miami, the Ocean Beach Resort and Spa was ending. I was still adjusting to losing my dad, now I would be losing my job, my hotel family, and the place that felt like home every time I walked in the building.

When no one else would hire me, they did. They knew I had little experience, yet they still thought I deserved a shot because of the excitement and eagerness I displayed during the interview. Once I was hired, the hotel team members adopted me as their daughter and little sister, often making sure I had a way home and checking on me on my days off. I truly felt they were a new family, a group of people who greatly cared about each other's well-being before anything else. The team who'd given me a promotion and believed in me was separating. Everyone and everything I knew was leaving me just as I was getting settled and confident in this life.

Pope Paul IV *(inspiringquotes.us, n.d)* once said, "Somebody should tell us, right at the start of our lives, that we are dying. Then we might live life to the limit, every minute of every day. Do it, I say.

Whatever you want to do, do it now! There are only so many tomorrows."

The first time I read that quote was after I learned I'd need to find a new job due to the renovations. It was the same month I discovered I was the executor to my dad's will. I was grateful my mom was now living only an hour and a half away from me as she would be crucial in helping me plan the funeral. I needed something to give me focus and power while most of me only wanted to crumble into a ball. I needed a plan. I went to bed, and when I woke up, I became obsessed with success. Pope Paul IV's quote reminded me how short life was and how much I still wanted to accomplish. Relaxing by the pool just felt like a waste of time. I needed to do it all right now. This started by making my dad proud no matter what. I went to work, marched up to my boss, and told her I'd made my decision. I was going to become a front office supervisor or manager and work toward becoming the general manager he knew I could be. I never stopped to ask myself what I really wanted in regard to my career.

Instead, I went to the job fair being hosted due to the hotel's closing and demanded each representative speak with me. I obtained three interview opportunities. The next week, I met with all the hotels. Of the three, only one wanted to offer me a leadership position. I didn't look at which location I'd receive the best training or which had the type of culture I valued. I kept thinking, "I must be promoted." I needed to become a general manager.

I wasn't feeling excited because when I'd met with the managers at the hotel that had the supervisor job available, they seemed very serious and not open to new ideas. At first, I turned down the offer, thinking I wanted a job that felt right. The first hotel I had worked at in the company had gained my trust, though, and I didn't want to start all over in a new company. I also didn't want to settle for an entry level, front desk agent offer. After a few weeks, against my better judgement, I emailed the human resources representative to ask if the supervisor position was still available. She replied that it was. I felt as if my options were limited and told myself to take the higher position and figure it out from there. Often when we start our careers, there's a take-what-you-can-get mentality, and what you believe is truly right for you gets pushed to the side.

Work and growing my career took on a bigger role. Focusing on work was my way of feeling I had some control in my world, which had been suddenly turned upside down. Having one place to channel my energy and determination helped, yet at times, I'd see someone who reminded me of my dad, and I'd be hit with the most intense pain. I pretended the pain didn't exist, and at night, I'd cry myself to sleep. I'd struggle with not being given the opportunity to say goodbye and not having had a chance to resolve our relationship for many years to come.

To cope, I created a fake identity of "South Beach Sue" to cover up for my life not being perfect. This persona was carefree and fun, always smiling. She was how I wanted to feel, and I believed if I pretended long enough maybe I could eventually become her. Social media would tell you I had the perfect life. Secretly, though, I knew that wasn't the case. Yet, rarely in movies and TV did I see people my age struggling. I felt ashamed to let anyone see that part of me. Instead,

I chose avoidance, thinking if I didn't tell anyone I was having a hard time, it would magically get better.

Transformative Tip #6

Why do you choose your current town to live in or do the job that you do? Is it what you truly want, or do you make your decisions based on what society suggests or your parents want for you, or maybe what your peers are doing? Remember you only have one life and the only person you need to impress is you. When you ask parents what they really want deep inside, the answer is usually for their children to be happy. We tell ourselves they will only be proud of me if... Spoiler! Even if your parents are not proud of you, even if they totally disagree with your life choices, it doesn't matter. Your being proud of yourself will take you anywhere you want to go in life. If you're not sure which path to take, go off somewhere quiet, preferably in nature. Close your eyes. Then ask the sky and trees your question. Look deep inside of you. Think about what makes you feel the most proud, happy, and alive. Then open your eyes and write down what answers feel most aligned to you. Do not judge or label the answer as right or wrong. If it feels right for you, it is. The only person you need to make happy is yourself.

CHAPTER 7: PAUSE AND INVEST IN YOURSELF

By August of 2007, life was starting to feel more predictable and dependable again. It wasn't that I'd forgotten my dad or no longer felt pain from his loss. Instead, his death gave me purpose to make the most of my life. I decided to plan a trip to Las Vegas for my twenty-fifth birthday! I invited my college friends from New York and my new Miami friends, and a few people from each group agreed to join the celebration. I started my new job as a front desk supervisor, and I was making a strong impact. I decided within a year I'd apply for a promotion. I became more and more involved in the South Beach social scene, and I still felt like a dream had come true as my email inbox quickly filled up with party invites.

I attended a work training seminar at a beautiful hotel in Fort Lauderdale and was feeling pretty happy with life and my progress. As I was driving home, my phone rang incessantly. I was driving on a highway and felt annoyed and overwhelmed, driving at sixty-five miles an hour. Finally, I took a deep breath and decided to answer it. My younger brother, Rob, was on the line and talking a mile a minute.

I couldn't make out the words. All I heard was "killed himself" and "Richard."

I don't know how I drove home, and I don't remember the other cars. It felt like there was no air. All I remember is hearing him say what I couldn't accept. My older brother, the one who would pick me up from parties when I needed saving, had killed himself. He was always laughing, smiling, teasing me to brush my teeth or they would fall out. He would flash his shiny, pearly whites after cracking a joke, and I'd feel loved. Richard or Richie as many of his friends called him had a certain Zen to him, and people seemed to relax in his presence. I admired his playing guitar and traveling with friends. He took life in stride. It just wasn't possible. I felt this sense of shame wash over me, but I didn't know why. I parked my car and threw myself on my bed. I didn't call any of my friends as I was trying to piece it all together.

I kept thinking back to the last time I saw him when he was in Miami for work. I had met him at his hotel, feeling important because he was inviting me to hang out with his coworkers. Being ten years older, he'd never included me because I was always his kid sister. I always thought he and his friends were cool, and I was honored he wanted them to meet me. I felt so proud and excited. I went to the hotel and hung out for a few hours. He asked if I'd join them out, but I had to work the next day and declined. My heart told me to join them, but my head said I had to be up at 7 a.m. He walked me out, but my gut told me something wasn't right. I don't know what it was, but it felt very final. I told him I loved him and walked home in the pouring rain as the tears streamed down my face.

I kept replaying that day over and over in my head, as once again, my face was wet from tears, this time due to my gut feelings from months ago unfortunately coming to fruition. The next few days went by in a blur, I remember calling my boss, struggling to tell her what happened as I boarded a flight from Miami to New York. It's been said the pain someone feels when they commit suicide is only passed on to those they love, and that was certainly the case for me. What made it worse was I couldn't really talk to my family about it. I didn't want to add to their sorrow with my own needs. Each of us grieved separately, and I never felt so alone.

Suicide in 2007 had such a stigma. When I lost my dad, I healed by writing dedications to him on social media and being with my feelings. Losing someone to suicide is very different. You're afraid people will judge you or religious people will tell you that committing suicide is a sin. Choosing to give up your life is such a taboo that the paper will often not mention the cause of death. This leaves the survivors, the family left behind, to feel a sense of shame because their loved one made that choice. I felt uncomfortable and had no idea how to navigate this loss, the loss of someone still so young.

I landed in New York and hugged my sister when she picked me up. We sat in silence in the car, both still in shock. I then wheeled my suitcase into my sister's house and started to listen to what the next few days held. No one seemed to know what to do first. My mom was wailing and crying, my sister kept looking through thousands of pictures, and my four-year-old niece just kept saying, "Tio? Tio? Tio?"

My sister told me he'd left a suicide note and let me read it.

He wrote, "I have been feeling gut wrenching pain for a long time and have only survived as long as I did from the love of my family and friends that became family."

That struck me hard because he seemed like such a down-to-earth person, one who was always smiling. I just didn't understand. People who were depressed stayed in bed and cried all day, didn't they?

Carpools of people from New York City showed up at the funeral, and with Christine's help, so did many of my high school and college friends. In Miami Beach, where he lived in his late twenties and early thirties, crowds gathered to honor him as well. For many of us, this was the first person we knew who died from a battle with depression, and he was only thirty-four. As people interacted, they all shared their conversations with him weeks and months before his suicide and tried to piece together how it ended this way.

He was cremated and wished to have his ashes thrown off a mountain in upstate New York. My sister placed the urn with his ashes inside of a white-painted wooden carton that had huge red hearts glued onto it. His friends offered to carry it, as it was heavy, but he was my brother, so I had to be the one to carry him up that mountain. I would internalize his heavy pain and feel a pressure on my heart constantly. We all gathered and said a few words, and I experienced everyone's pain combined with my own. I heard a guttural, almost animal-like wail, and when I looked up, I saw it was coming from my mom. I wished I had more than one body because I didn't know who to comfort first. The only relief came when someone showed a portrait they'd drawn of him while making a heartfelt dedication.

My niece in her little voice cried out, "There you are, Tio! Tio, I love you."

As we climbed down the mountain, it was even harder because in our own ways, each person blamed themselves for not doing more, for not seeing the signs, and for not helping him and checking on him. The more I saw him through his friends' eyes, the more I loved him. My mind raced a mile a minute, and everything felt heavy. Eventually, it was over. Then, I realized I had a flight booked to Vegas in just a few days. I talked to my mom and sister about it as I didn't feel right going. They convinced me the best way to honor him was to go on the trip. My friends were counting on me, and he lived his life for the present moment. During the trip, I pushed away my feelings. I wanted to make him proud by living the best life possible, and that started with having the time of my life in Vegas.

I know you may be thinking: *Her brother just died, and she is living it up in Vegas?*

Part of me felt it was wrong, but I was craving any sense of being a normal twenty-five-year-old that I could. I wanted to be someone else, anyone else, so I would go out pre-party and drink a ton until I could no longer feel. With tears running down my face, I'd dance and meet random men, hoping for something that would heal the aching pain. I honestly don't know how much I told my friends that came on the trip about losing my brother or if I even told them about losing him at all. Instead, I trained my brain to focus on the positives.

I wasn't going to let anything stop me from feeling alive. He used to make fun of me, saying I'd study and work too hard, and I kept thinking he'd want me to have fun. While I felt a part of me died with him, I dug deep and faked my feelings to convince others that I was happy. While this was exhausting, it was easier than having to answer constant questions or retell the story of what had happened.

I felt wrong and guilty partying, yet part of me appreciated doing something normal, something I did before my world was turned upside down. I focused on my friends and having a good time in Vegas, hoping Richard would look down and be proud of me.

I never asked myself the question: *Are you okay?*

I knew if I actually stopped and examined my feelings, I may never have recovered, so I pushed myself to enjoy the trip and focus on appreciating that my friends had come from multiple states to be there with me. By the time I got home, I thought of my dad and brother and was conflicted. Do I focus on my career, working hard, and moving up the ladder, or do I focus on my social needs and spending time with my friends and the Meetin.org group?

I thought about having people over to my apartment as I did after my dad's death, sitting shiva, which is the time of mourning in the Jewish tradition after someone passes. This time, though, it didn't feel right. I felt ashamed. When people would ask about how my dad passed, and I'd reply, "A heart attack," they would nod and tell me how sorry they were. When people asked about my brother's passing, there was always an awkward silence.

"He killed himself, oh my!"

I hated being the source of discomfort, so I stopped telling people or talking about it. I just wanted to be done with 2007, this year of unexpected pain and disconnection from my peers.

In my mind, there was a *before 2007* and an *after 2007* Sue, and I was never to be the same again. I'd grown up overnight. The hardest part was how little mental health and suicide was talked about back then. As I met new people and dated, they'd ask how many siblings I have, and I never knew what to say. If I mentioned him, they would ask questions about where he lived and what he did. I would find myself not wanting to lie, yet when I told them the truth, that I had a brother who was no longer with us, there was only an awkward pause. If I said I just had two siblings, I felt I was lying to myself, and it was as if he died all over again.

My family continued to avoid talking about it. I'd see my friends and how I made them smile, and the last thing I wanted to be was the person who brought them down, so I made a decision to lock up my true self. I never mentioned him and how I was struggling. Instead, I focused on acting as a leader at work and a social organizer with my friends. The more I tried, the harder it got. I started to disappear mentally and emotionally, yet I was still physically social. Constantly, I thought about just staying in bed, about giving up, about never waking up again. I knew, though, that if I let myself stay in bed or on the couch and stop going out with my friends, my family would worry, so I put on a happy face. I truly believed that if I just kept focusing on everyone else, somehow their happiness would flow into me. This method, also known as toxic positivity, tries to focus on the positives and reject the negatives, is commonly experienced by many achievers. Medicalnewstoday, *Medicalnewstoday.com:Toxic positivity: Definition, risks, how to avoid, and more 2021)* defines toxic positivity as "an obsession with positive thinking. Toxic positivity can silence negative emotions, demean grief, and make people feel under pressure to pretend to be happy even when they are struggling."

Please understand it's not that I didn't examine the idea of getting professional help. I just didn't want to label myself as someone who needed help or give off the impression something was wrong with me. My outlook of toxic positivity impacted all the areas of my life. I became a master at hiding how I really felt from not only other people but myself as well. Ever since graduating, I had been working hard to prove I didn't need anyone to take care of me. By seeing a therapist, or saying I needed help, I would be saying I was not enough. I would be admitting I needed to rely on other people. In addition, I would suddenly be different than everyone I knew. At twenty-five, the main need you have is to belong, to create friendship groups, to have happy hours with coworkers. I didn't want to be the damaged girl who lost her dad and brother. I was at the age where my friends' biggest problems were how weird their last date was. I wasn't prepared to deal with such tremendous losses so quickly. After my dad, I called my company's resource line, and they sent me grief CDs to listen to. It was a short-term band aid, but it got me to focus on the now.

After losing Richard, I went to a suicide support group, but after a few weeks of greeting the new members and hearing their stories of loss, I found it was hurting more than helping. I envisioned one on one therapy sessions as living in the past repeatedly telling the story of what had happened with my dad and brother and didn't think a therapist could be of much help. In my mind, coping was living. If I could survive, that was enough. Getting out of bed was an accomplishment. Showering was another accomplishment. Waking up and leaving the house became my definition of being alive. Meanwhile, on social media, all my friends thought I was having the time of my life. I posted photos of the beach and the nightlife just to see how many likes I would get, and I'd feel a secret thrill every time I logged in and saw how many people responded to my pictures. I learned how to walk the walk and talk the talk, and as the years went on, my outfits got shorter and more revealing, and more and more men gave me attention—men who just ten years ago never would've looked my way. I found myself craving their attention and felt a hole in my heart where my dad and brother used to be.

Transformative Tip #7:

Have you ever avoided dealing with something negative that occurred in your life? After a traumatic event, it's common to try to do everything other than process what you'd experienced. I chose to stay occupied and distracted, so the day went by faster. Often you just want life to go back to "normal," so you attempt to return to your previous life—the life you once knew, the one that happened before the incident. Unfortunately, life will never be the same and that's okay. Neither are you. Every moment in life helps us in our growth.

When we physically exercise, we often have moments in which we need to catch our breath. Sometimes the workout is too much for us to handle, and we need to pause. The same is true for our lives. When you feel that too much is going on in your life, or you are having a hard time processing or understanding something, it's a clear sign you need to pause. Take a few days or a leave from work. Say no to some social plans. Take a social media break. Speak to someone who can help you create a plan for your healing. Go to a park or beach. Stop. Just pause. Stop, breathe, and feel. Sometimes the simplest life can be the best life. Become comfortable calling a timeout. The world will still be there after you have taken time to make yourself the top priority.

CHAPTER 8: FEEL IT TO HEAL IT

As 2007 ended, Miami was booming. Occupancy at my hotel was at an all-time high. I embraced the business, as it was a welcome distraction from my thinking about the fact that half of my family was gone. I took pride in each guest who left happy and thanked me for my help. I was no longer Mel's daughter or Richard's sister. Without them, I felt I'd lost my compass. I felt completely disconnected from myself. I regretted not appreciating them enough when they were alive. Everyone kept telling me I couldn't have done anything to help them, but I just didn't believe it. I wanted to feel something, anything other than the numbing pain, but all I could do was do my best to avoid real, vulnerable connections.

I carried around a sense of guilt that I should live and breathe while my dad and brother no longer could. I went back and forth between working hard to be successful while making this life count to thinking we're all going to die anyway, nothing really matters, and I may as well live hedonistically in the moment. Living in the moment meant not thinking about the consequences, engaging in risky behaviors both sexually and with alcohol. I stopped caring, stopped respecting myself, and just kept fighting to try to stay positive.

I looked outward to feel like I was enough. I would feel a thrill when I got into a free event or partied with a celebrity. I truly thought that would be enough. If I could just look happy, I convinced myself I would be. Maybe if I could disappear who I really was and buy into this superficial life, I would be okay. If I could just stop feeling, if I could just let go, I could manage! Going out and drinking and dancing until the sun came up and then passing out for a few hours before work became my routine. It was probably not the healthiest, but it did become a source of comfort and certainty, a sense I had something in my life I could depend upon.

Walking into a club, hearing the click of the velvet rope open was like an entry into an alternate universe. Here everyone was smiling—happy. You could do anything with anyone, and it was accepted. We were young, we were beautiful, and we were alive. I would close my eyes and try to shut out my crazy workday and the pain I was feeling from my losses. I would concentrate on the beat of the music and for a few hours take a vacation from my life and nonstop brain activity. I was living in a place people waited years to visit, and the beaches and clubs were my backyard. In my gut though, I knew the heavy, bad parts of life were not over nor could I ignore my pain forever. Part of me was aware, but I didn't want to stop and deal with the debilitating emotions. I was anxious for what was to come and would wonder who I might lose next.

Work became busier and busier as we entered what was known as "the season," the months between November to April, when people escaped the cold plaguing the rest of North America and Europe. I left work anywhere from 12 a.m. to 1 a.m., as there was always some guest issue that needed attention at the last moment. Often, as I was about to leave, we would get a call from our partner company that handled cancelled flight passengers. Suddenly, I would look up from my computer and see the shuttles of people arriving at the hotel. Cancelled flights could never be predicted, and I became frustrated that no matter how much I planned my night to leave on time, if that call came, I didn't feel right leaving our overnight team, including the manager, Ted, to deal with this surge alone. When you are in a twenty-four-hour industry, you never close. Part of me thrived off the energy, having so many people who "needed" me, whether it was my front desk staff or the many guests with questions and concerns. I was so busy, I stopped making plans with my friends and instead would go out with my coworkers since they were free on weeknights.

One March weekend, I finally was off from work! It was a big deal to have a weekend when I wasn't working. I had become used to working while others were having fun. The only people I wanted to spend it with were my Meetin.org friends since I hadn't seen them in a while. As luck would have it, one of the social groups I was in was hosting an event with two-for-one drinks until midnight. This event was located at a club downtown, so my friend Brenda and I took a taxi from South Beach. This was a big deal in the eighteen-dollars-a-drink world of Miami. It was the most beautiful night all around: weather, people, and energy. I was home. I belonged. I was going to have the best night! I had a few drinks, danced, laughed, and felt at peace. I looked around and had a flashback, one of a similar party only three years earlier.

Do you remember my first Miami party? The one I left crying because I felt so out of place? I closed my eyes and felt an overwhelming sense of gratitude that I had stayed in this city. In a few years, I matured and grew up in so many ways. I met people from all over the world, learned how to budget my money, lived alone, and created a routine of work and fun. I had envisioned and delivered a new life for myself. I had worked my way up from an entry level front desk agent. Now, I was in a leadership role at a hotel. I no longer felt like a kid playing dress up. Instead, I belonged in the Miami social scene and was even the planner for most of my friends' weekends. I networked and was allowed entrance into places I never imagined, like the Versace Mansion or parties on private islands. I looked around at the beautiful people. I saw my friends' smiling faces, and I realized one of my greatest strengths was connecting people. I realized Miami may have been a change and a challenge, but I had learned so many life lessons already. One powerful take away was that confidence can get you anything you want. I knew exactly what I needed to focus on in order to get my goals accomplished: trust in myself and self-confidence.

As the night went on, I lost myself in the music. I loved the fact that Miami clubs stayed open until 6 a.m., and I could leave whenever I wanted rather than being forced out by an early closing time. Wandering the club like I owned the place, I saw people I knew in every corner. It was truly amazing. A few hours later, as I was dancing, Brenda told me she was heading home and asked if I wanted to leave. *Leave?* Was she crazy? The DJ was great, drinks were flowing, and the crowd was fun. No, I did not want to leave. I wanted to soak up the good memories. I recently had too many bad ones. Now was my time, and I deserved to see what twenty-six was all about. As Pitbull wrote *(Pitbill & Christina, 2012)*, "I just want (ed) to feel this moment." I was staying! I wish this was where my story ended, but it was about to take a really terrible turn.

I don't remember too much after that, but from what I can piece together, I met a guy from Chicago, originally from Israel. We danced, and he offered to buy me another drink. I must have blacked out because the next thing I knew, I was in a cab with this guy and his six friends, both male and female. They were talking really loudly, and I heard my inner voice saying, "This isn't the way home."

I struggled and panicked, but no words came out. It was like my mind and body were separate from each other. I felt so tired after getting out of the cab. It was like trying to walk in quicksand. My body felt so heavy, and I thought maybe if I just took a quick nap, I'd be able to get the energy to call a cab home. I followed the group to the condo they were renting for the weekend, still trying to get my bearings.

After walking in, the group separated into different bedrooms. Not sure where to go, I waited in the living room while everyone else dispersed. I dragged myself to the nearest piece of furniture, a sofa chair, and started to close my eyes. I was almost asleep when I woke up to someone kissing me and rubbing their hands up and down my body. I mumbled, "Please, I just want to sleep. I'm so tired I just need sleep." I groaned, moved away from him, and hoped he would go away if I ignored him.

The more I told him no, the weaker I got. It was like I was a balloon slowly deflating. The idea of getting up and getting away was just not an option, and I felt my eyes flutter as I fell asleep. This time the touching went under my dress on my stomach and in my underwear. Something in me knew I had to create strength where there was none. I pushed him off me, quickly grabbed my shoes, and ran toward the door, feeling my breathing getting faster. Upon opening the door, I felt a sense of relief that I had gotten out! I opened the heavy door and bam, thud! I tripped, fell, and passed out. It pains me to describe what happened next.

All I can remember is looking down and watching myself. It was surreal, I wondered if I was dead. I knew I was floating yet I wasn't in a pool. *Is this what heaven feels like?* But I knew it didn't feel peaceful, so what was going on? The experience of being out of your body and seeing yourself is truly indescribable. I knew it was me, yet I had no body, no form—just awareness that something felt wrong. I felt trapped as I watched myself lying there.

Then I felt him pushing inside me and I knew something was really wrong. I was caged inside of my own body. I kept yelling at myself, "Sue, wake up! Sue, get away from him! Sue, don't be weak! Sue, *fight!*" I thought about screaming, but I was scared what he would do if I tried. It was around 5 a.m. and people were fast asleep. Who was going to hear me? I experienced a variety of panicked thoughts and solutions, yet my body and voice weren't able to take any action! Finally, I had a thought: I could give up and die, or I could try to act. My need to survive kicked into full force. I managed to push him off of me, grabbed my purse and shoes, and ran like an Olympian to the elevator. I honestly don't know if my feet touched the floor. I ran and ran. As I got up, I left a part of me on that floor. I pounded the elevator button, looked back, pounded the elevator button again, and looked back again. The thought crossed my mind that maybe this was how my life ended. What if he came after me and grabbed me and flung me onto the floor? What if it happened again?

My mind was flooded with thoughts, and I felt a deep sense of panic in my heart. It truly felt like it was breaking. I clutched my shoes in one hand and my purse in the other as I heard him get up. Finally, the doors opened, and I breathed a big sigh of relief. I had survived.

My cell phone must have been dead because I remember asking the front desk person to call me a cab. As I was waiting, I noticed three surveillance camera screens behind him, and I felt the need to remember that fact. I was me, but I felt like I was in a weird fog state. My whole body felt tight like I was a robot. Even opening my mouth to speak proved difficult. After what seemed like forever, the cab showed up. I gave my address and sat in complete silence. I never felt so sad, broken, and drained in my entire life. I looked out the window trying to figure out what time it was. The sun was coming up, so I assumed it was about 6:30 a.m. I couldn't shake the frozen, numb feeling. After about twenty-five minutes, I arrived home. The cab only took cash, and I had just enough for the sixty-dollar tab. I found my key, slowly opened the door, and collapsed in my bed and wept. Finally, I could sleep.

In what seemed like no time at all, I found myself slowly blinking my eyes and taking in my surroundings. The first observation I had was it was now dark, and I was feeling disoriented. I had been drunk before, and I knew this was more than that. *What time was it? How did I get here? What happened last night?* I didn't wake up hungover; I woke up lost. I kept replaying what happened over and over in my head. My mind just couldn't make sense of it. Twenty-four hours ago, I had been trying on half my wardrobe for a fun night out with friends. Now I was waking up feeling like I couldn't function. Was it my fault? Did I have too much to drink? Was it *that* bad? How could that have happened? What did I do wrong? What do I do now?

One thought came to my mind: call Christine. So, I did, and I started to cry as soon as she picked up.

She kept asking me, "Sue, what's wrong? Sue, talk to me."

I just kept crying as there were no words to explain. I still didn't know what happened, only that in my core something felt very wrong. I took a deep breath, closed my eyes, and told her everything I could recall.

She said "Sue, you were raped."

My mind immediately went into fight mode. Raped? No, I couldn't have been raped. I was a sweet girl, brought up in a nice family, and went to a good school. Things like that didn't happen to me.

But she said in the sternest, most straight-forward voice I've ever heard, "Sue, you need to go to the hospital. Call a friend and have them take you. Promise me you will go. Bring the dress you wore."

She would not get off the phone with me until I told her I'd call someone. I hung up and said to myself, "It's okay, don't listen to her. It's not that big of a deal, just go back to bed." I was tempted to obey, but then I heard my voice telling her that I promised. The first person who came into my head wasn't the friend I'd gone out with that night or any of my Meetin.com friends, but one of my coworkers, Irina, whom I always saw as tough and strong. We'd hung out after work a few times. I called her, and she picked up right away. "Suzie, it's 10 p.m., are you okay?"

This time I didn't cry. I said I need to go to the hospital because something bad happened. She didn't ask any questions, and in twenty minutes she was outside my apartment. We rode in silence the whole time.

At the hospital's emergency room, I numbly filled out the forms. When the nurse called my name to go into the exam room, Irina asked if I wanted her to come in with me.

I had already felt embarrassed for calling her as she wasn't a close friend, so I quietly whispered, "It's okay, I'll be okay." I don't know if I said this more for her benefit or if I was trying to convince myself. I didn't make eye contact with her and stared at the floor instead. After that, I don't remember much other than a male police officer taking my statement and the doctor doing a quick exam. I was then told there was another local hospital that was an expert location for rape cases, and they were referring me there. The officer and I exited the room.

Irina walked over, heard what was going on, and asked if she needed to take me to the next hospital. The officer said not to worry, and he would take me, and with that, I was alone. I felt very uncomfortable in the back of a police car sitting in silence with the officer. All my senses were on guard. He told me this happened all the time in Miami, and because I didn't know the assailant's name and only knew that he raped me in a beachfront condo building with "ocean" in the name, they would probably never find him.

This made me want to open up the doors and run away. I felt I was wrong for wasting his time on a case that would probably never be brought to trial. I felt like the criminal, like he was going with me because he had to, even though he knew there was no point in my reporting. We went to the second hospital, located in a neglected area of downtown Miami, and it was awful. As we were waiting for me to be seen, I couldn't ignore the drug addicts and homeless people next to me. The doctor and police officer kept grilling me with questions, feeling no empathy, and I had to keep repeating my story to the point where I wondered if it happened. They gave me a rape kit and ran all different kinds of tests. I was told to get dressed and given a tri-fold paper pamphlet with resources for help. The officer asked if I wanted to drive around and try to find the building, but since this was hours later, I was drained and had tolerated enough. I told him I just wanted to sleep, so he drove me home.

Trembling, I opened the door of his car and slammed it shut. I walked into my apartment and plopped down on the couch. I couldn't even make it to my bed. My heart wouldn't stop beating out of my chest. I dropped the pamphlet on my table and didn't want to look at it, avoiding having to admit what happened was real. It finally hit me that something really bad occurred, and I had a role in it. What made it really hurt was that I felt I couldn't tell my mom or sister. It was just six months after losing my brother, and they were still very much grieving, so we were pretty distant. I would not bring them more pain. I knew they would only ask me why I didn't go home with my friends, why I was drinking, and why I was staying out so late.

The next day was Monday, and work was waiting for me. I probably should have called and told them I couldn't make it in, but the only days I took off were when I lost my dad and brother. I wouldn't allow this incident to be of the same scale of importance in my life. I knew I would be helping by going to work, making a difference to my staff and the guests. I thought that I would be with people rather than with my mind filled with thoughts. Most importantly, I was craving routine and needed familiarity. I went through my work prep routine on autopilot, knowing no difference between the water from the shower and the tears raining down on my face. I was all alone.

Upon arriving at work, I realized that while so much had changed for me, the hotel was still the same. As soon as I walked in, I was bombarded with a million questions and requests and felt completely numb and overwhelmed. I finally worked up the courage to knock on my boss's door. I was shaking and crying. My boss, Jessica, asked me what was wrong. I slunk into the chair, avoiding eye contact. I told her I'd been assaulted. Like with many victims, the word "rape" was just too hard to say.

"Did it happen at work?" she asked. When I shook my head, I started to cry even more. Suddenly, I felt a surge of strength, and the entire story spilled out of my mouth. My heart was craving for someone I could trust who would make it all better. She responded, "I see. Do you want to go home or stay and work?"

I was immediately transported back to my first day at work after Vegas, when the team had given me a blanket and a card to support me through the loss of my brother. I remembered the compassion, the care, and mostly the sense of belonging to an extended family. When you work crazy hours with guests screaming at you, you make magic somehow, and the staff becomes people you see through the good and bad in life. I thought about myself that morning, crying in the shower, and thought with a sinking feeling that if I went home, someone else would need to stay late. I was in no shape to make any decisions other than putting one foot in front of the other.

My manager stated, "If you're going to stay, then go to the bathroom, wash your face, and come back." And with that, I was dismissed.

The first time I saw my friends after the rape, I had a hard time making eye contact. I knew I had a secret, and I was accustomed to telling my friends everything. Unfortunately, opening up to Irina and Jessica about what happened had been incredibly uncomfortable and painful. I couldn't stand the idea of any of my close friends looking at me with pity or seeing me as someone different than them. People saw me as the happy go lucky social butterfly. I couldn't imagine being the one to share such tragic news with them. I only wanted to belong. Working a different schedule than most of my friends had caused a small gap, but I would email my schedule to them weekly to try to bridge this and create closeness. Losing my dad, when no one really could understand, added to this feeling of being unlike my peers. Having to say goodbye to my brother when my friends were focused on dating and their careers made me cling to light topics at brunch such as guys and parties. Rape, though, would create an even bigger wedge, one I wasn't willing to risk. There was nothing my friends could do to fix what happened, and there was no need to keep the most awful story of my life alive on repeat.

According to mentalhealthdaily.com, (*mentalhealthdaily, At what age is the brain fully developed? 2015*), by the ages of twenty-five and twenty-six, humans are said to have a fully matured prefrontal cortex, the area of the brain that controls our ability to make choices and moral decisions. Experiencing sexual assault tears you apart not only physically and emotionally but also mentally as well. So, this begs the question: what happens to people's decision-making abilities who experience immense traumas at or before this particular age?

In my case, I wasn't sure who to turn to, who to trust, who to confide in. I was still trying to process what had happened from the scattered snapshots in my mind. As much as I cared about my friends, I was a bit apprehensive to trust them again. I wondered when they would leave me when I needed a friend. I also was upset at myself for trusting this guy to get me a drink. I didn't know who to blame, and in many ways, I clung to denial. Pushing past the assault and my feelings surrounding it would allow me to have my life back. Every time I thought about what happened, it would only upset me more, and the idea of telling people, while holding my breath in anticipation of how they'd respond was just too much. I thought, in time, the nightmares would go away, and I would feel like me again. They say time heals all wounds, right? I just needed time to work its magic.

As a society, we're not taught how to handle someone sharing details about a tragedy. When good things happen like weddings or promotions, we easily know what to do and say. "Congratulations! I'm proud of you!"

When sad or uncomfortable things happen, we just say things like, "I'm sorry to hear that. Sorry for your loss." We respond in a way that's safe and comfortable to us. Rarely do people ask questions such as: *Are you ok? Do you want to talk about it? When you're ready to talk about your mom, brother, etc., I'd love to listen. Is there anything I can do for you?* Why is this not taught to us in school as we are growing up? Why are we lacking articles on supporting those in our community who are struggling?

Oh, that's right, it's all about self-help. We're expected to help ourselves. I was told, "You should seek help." This sounds like an easy solution, yet we forget the impact the trauma may have had on a person. It takes so much strength to trust a complete stranger after being sexually violated or having your heart ripped out. This is why we need to be there for each other. If someone ever confides in you that they're struggling or stressed, please see this as a gift because it's so much easier to keep feelings inside.

The way the first few people respond to a sexual assault claim can directly impact a victim's recovery experience. So, what could my manager have done in this situation? According to RAINN.org (Rape, Abuse, Incest National Network), (*Tips for Talking with Survivors of Sexual Assault | RAINN*, 2019) here are some ways she could've done better:

"I believe you. It took a lot of courage to tell me about this."

"It's not your fault. You didn't do anything to deserve this."

"You are not alone. I care about you, and I'm here to listen or help in any way I can."

"I'm sorry this happened. This shouldn't have happened to you."

Since I wasn't met with an empathetic response, I had no choice but to feel like I was making a big deal out of nothing. I pasted a smile on my face and disappeared. A new coping mechanism was born. In the past, my way of surviving was to just keep going. With this "keep going" mentality, I was still present in my life, but I was not dealing with the past. "Just keeping going" was no longer possible because it felt like a battle in my head every time I tried to stay focused and present in my life. Instead, I just mentally disappeared. I became an expert at physically being somewhere surrounded by dozens of people, but mentally being somewhere far, far away in a safe land where no one could hurt me, and I didn't really have to feel.

After a while, I felt my protective shield was a permanent part of my body. A new Sue was born while the real Sue was dying inside of a shell. If she could just stay happy, she could perfect the power of disappearing the moment people got too close, so she didn't have to risk trusting them. This fake person seemed like she had hundreds of friends, but she was secretly hiding a deep, dark secret.

Two days later, I got a call from the police. My report was ready. I drove there with a mix of both excitement and dread. Part of me thought it would be over if I could just get the report and file it away like a bad test grade. As I approached the police station, I was anxious and felt my hands stiffen, but I told myself to just get the report and be done. A police officer asked me for my ID, and I felt my stomach tighten because I never liked being in police stations or hospitals. Even though I wasn't at fault, I still felt scared. She printed a copy of the report for me and told me to have a good day. I was proud of myself for how well I was handling it.

I started to think about my evening plans, but something was nagging at me. I needed to know what the report said even though I knew it was probably not a good idea to read it. I slowly opened the white folded paper and quickly scanned it. Certain lines jumped out at me: *Didn't know the building... mentioned ocean in name... barely speaking... didn't know his name.* I was immediately crushed. I've never felt so much like I didn't matter before, like I was just a number, and it became clear I had no case.

I kept hearing the officer's voice in my head: "It happens all the time, all the time, all the time!"

If it happened *all the time,* who was I to be different? Why would they believe me? Why would they care? I had clear evidence on the building's camera footage, yet I felt overwhelmed, exhausted, and like a statistic from that day on. I was just another file on the floor next to the officer's desk. The more I saw myself as a dirty file with a coffee stain on top, the more upset I became. I had reached the *anger* stage. My heart and head felt like they were going to explode, and I felt the blood coursing through my body.

That's when it happened. I was walking outside, looked across the street, and I saw the building. I knew it in my bones, and I froze and crumbled. Like a freight train, my memories flooded back, and I felt so powerless, I fell to the floor. My immediate thought was that bad things come in threes. Memories of my dad's funeral and my brother's memorial came rushing back. At first, I shook my head and whispered, "Maybe I'm just cursed." I was so angry at everyone involved. The rapist, my friend, and the police. My entire brain felt like it was being pulled apart.

Then a voice—I'm not sure if it was God or my dad or brother or my gut—said, "Sue, you are not quitting yet!"

At that moment, I made a promise to myself. Somehow, the promises you make to yourself feel more important but aren't as easily kept. I closed my eyes and promised myself, "He will not win. I will not let him ruin my life!"

I know you may be wondering why I didn't turn around and tell the police. I was just too scared. I was worried that no matter how much I remembered, they wouldn't believe me. I was afraid of being seen as damaged to my friends and family. I was petrified to be anywhere near *him* again. I often think of the song lyric from Just the Two of Us, by Will Smith (Smith, 1998) "Throughout life people will make you mad. Disrespect you and treat you bad. Let G-d deal with the things they do cause hate in your heart will consume you too." On a conscious level I was trying to follow this advice, but unconsciously I was mad and resentful. I told myself I could let it go and get on with my life, but deep inside my subconscious, the bitterness only grew.

I convinced myself that pursuing the case would give him more power by taking time out of my life. Letting myself feel the awfulness of what had happened would mean I would have to stop. If I stopped, I believed to a certain extent I would never go again. I would shrivel up and die. I had survived, and I would take the world on by storm. He would only win if I gave up on life, but I was a fighter. I decided at that moment he was dead to me, and I wouldn't waste another moment thinking about what had happened. I declared myself as unstoppable.

I proceeded to go out dancing with those same friends just a week later. I promised myself I'd make sure he wouldn't stop me. I dressed up, straight ironed my hair, put on makeup, yet I couldn't seem to make eye contact with myself in the mirror. I started staying out later, drinking more, and working longer. I was going to have it all again. Yet, something felt off. I was no longer aligned with myself. As scary as it had been being alone with my rapist that night, it became just as scary to be alone with myself. Something we don't often talk about in regard to assault is how much victims stop trusting themselves. As much as I knew it wasn't my fault, my instincts and trust in myself were gone. I was a shell fighting to breathe and often gasping for air, constantly feeling someone was after me. I was anxious and hating myself.

I switched into a new, don't-mess-with-me, fighter Sue and would yell at my coworkers and even my mom for minor things. I would constantly feel my mind racing, and as soon as I got to the beach, I would pass out for hours at a time in the middle of the afternoon. I stopped knowing how to say "no," and when my boss would call to see if I could work because someone called in sick, I would drop everything to be there. Every single time, I would feel obligated to sacrifice and help. I became a little puppy who just needed love. I was desperate to feel needed.

We're conditioned to think people who are raped typically become depressed and pull away from others. They even jump at slightly being touched. That's the rape victim we're made to see. There's another response people often don't talk about, and that's the knee-jerk reaction I had. The response involves feeling like all you want is to take control back, but you're never able to connect and trust yourself enough to do so.

At work, I would tentatively speak up for myself but when met with even the least bit of resistance or push back I would quickly feel dejected and immediately give up. I knew no matter who I spoke to, no matter how much I tried to stick up for myself or a fellow coworker I would never win that discussion. My brain had a hard time pausing and seeing what solutions and resources were available to me. It was as if I were stuck in an alternate universe, one where the only role I knew to play was as a rape victim. Respect and communication and love no longer felt comfortable. After a while, self-expression and putting myself first were no longer achievable options. I did whatever the powerful people with authority in my life wanted me to do. I gave up and went into autopilot, just doing what was needed to get through the day. I had trouble focusing at work and would make mistakes. I told myself that was just how I was, never connecting my troubles to the trauma I'd experienced. I saw my being unorganized or struggling with small tasks as part of being in a busy workplace. I'd wake up in the middle of the night, clutching my heart, and gasping for breath filled with work nightmares of guests upset and yelling at me. It did cross my mind that maybe I should find a new job, but I wasn't a quitter. As I made more mistakes, my boss would often tell me I wasn't ready for the next step, and after a while, I believed her.

At work, I had a hard time trusting myself to speak up. At brunch, I didn't feel comfortable telling my friends how bad parts of my life really were. Even more inhibiting than feeling awkward, I didn't think

I knew how to share what I was experiencing. What words do you use to tell people you're struggling?

When I was with friends, I responded in three different ways when it came to my problems. The first was I'd only share the good, like a great new happy hour I found recently. I'd choose to focus on the positive, hoping I could convince my brain to be happy. The second, which I used less often, was I'd share my obstacles, but I'd downplay what I was dealing with. I'd only tell them some of my struggles. Maybe I'd mention my sleep was restless, and my friends would justify it because I was balancing multiple projects at work. I remember telling one friend that I found it weird I had very few memories, and she replied that everyone was different when it came to how much we remembered. After a while, I started to believe all of what I was going through could be explained and was normal. The third way, which happened for me rarely, was when my brain allowed me to be in the moment. A friend would make a comment or say a joke and I would feel full present and connected. A wave of gratitude would wash over me, and for a few minutes, I was able to feel all the love around me. Those days always caught me off guard. It took a lot to have the perfect recipe to be able to be fully present. Perhaps it was getting enough sleep, not running into work, or maybe it was more of a deliberate choice and would happen when I woke up choosing to have a good day and appreciate my life. Perhaps it was on those days, which would usually be when I was off for a weekend, I didn't take my time with my friends for granted. I allowed myself to give up the fear and truly allow myself to understand and enjoy the people around me.

Each day, though, when I woke up, I had no idea which of the three my brain would choose. What I did know is that when I went out, I'd feel connected to people and a part of something. In South Beach music, dancing was a way of life. It was a way of expressing yourself and a sense of belonging with people no matter their race, home city, sex, or sexual orientation. I didn't want to admit it, but I was searching for some glimmer of hope. I just wanted to escape reality and feel happy, and the dark nightclubs of South Beach allowed this. These venues became my home away from home, the one place I felt safe enough to use my voice. The DJs at the nightclubs would play music that reminded me other people struggled and rose above their obstacles. I'd hear the messages and the energy behind these songs, and no matter what the artists were dealing with, the theme was the same: it's ok to feel. The popular beats played on repeat and the words gave me a sense of consistency and familiarity. The next day society and my job would have power over me. I'd wake up every day guilty for feeling so weighed down by my emotions. But at whatever club was popular at the moment, I could lower my protective shield. I felt all the experiences these singers were entrusting me with. I let go, danced on couches, and kissed anyone I wanted. For a few brief hours, I felt alive, present, and free!

Being in my twenties in a worldwide party destination, the actions I took were seen as normal and my friends never questioned my late nights or choices. While I had to work weekends, I mainly worked the evening shifts, so I didn't have to worry about being late. Even if I stayed out until 6 a.m., I could easily make it to work by 3 p.m. It was the weekend, so no one told me I should drink less or go home earlier.

My friends and I would get invited to join a group of guys in the VIP section with free alcohol, or we'd know a promoter who'd get us in early with free drinks. It was just too easy. My friends were trying to let loose as much as I was. I had worked hard and behaved all through college, barely drinking or going out. Instead, I would stay in and study or watch a movie with my boyfriend. Now was my time to have fun, and there was always someone around who would be texting me asking what club or bar I was going to that night.

One time I was leaving a club and tripped and fell flat on my face in front of a crowd of people. You'd think that would've been enough to stop me, but there was this part of me that became addicted to being out. I needed to do whatever I could to feel free just for a moment, and alcohol allowed me to do that. I would wind up dancing with a guy and go home with him or take him to my apartment.

My mind was not there, only my body, so I was hoping if I consensually slept with enough men, it would somehow balance out the one time I didn't give permission. It would restore my power. Maybe one of those guys would actually care about me at some point. I was lucky to meet a few really good men who walked me home but declined coming in because they felt something was off. However, plenty of others took advantage of the opportunity. I no longer had to be completely conscious and present when it came to sex. On days I went home alone, I would end up passed out on the bathroom floor covered in my own vomit holding myself and crying. This was heart wrenching but became my norm. I didn't think much of myself and no longer thought a truly fulfilling life was possible.

My response was, "Well, at least I made it home."

I was determined to put a positive spin on whatever life was bringing me. I was living in a beautiful city with lots of family and friends close by. Work was hectic, but I really liked my coworkers. I wasn't even angry at my attacker anymore. I was mostly mad at myself because I didn't do more about it.

Now, when I think back to those times, I think about the cameras in the building where the rape occurred, and I know if someone had believed in me, we may have been able to find the building and see the tapes. I may not have gone down this path of destruction, giving myself over to whatever the nights would bring. I felt a bit like I was living three lives. The life most people thought I had living it up in Miami, the workaholic career woman, and the stay busy, never pause, stay on the go, hard to focus, panicked me. Whether it was waking up on the bathroom floor or waking up screaming in the middle of the night, I felt my life was spiraling out of control, and there was nothing I could do to escape. I believed I alone was experiencing this out-of-control anxiousness and wouldn't realize until much later these symptoms actually had a name: PTSD.

Post-Traumatic Stress Disorder (PTSD) was barely talked about at the time, and when it was, it only related to soldiers coming back from war. I had no idea I was in a battle all my own. I'll never forget what happened one night when my mom slept over. I had a nightmare and woke up with a jolt. In the dream, all the guests were yelling at me, and there was nothing I could do. My heart was pounding, and my pillow and sheets were covered in sweat. When I got up, I wanted to wake my mom and tell her I had a nightmare like when I was a kid. As I looked over and watched her slowly breathe in and out, I no longer saw her as this superhero who could make my bad dreams go away. Instead, she was only human and was still hurting from my brother's passing. I visualized waking her. I walked over and... I couldn't do it. I shook my head and tried to open my mouth, but something stopped me. In my mind, I knew she would only groggily ask me why I was up and tell me to go back to bed.

I thought about it one more time, and decided it was best to just go back to sleep. I'd feel better in the morning. The next day I looked up the meaning of dreams online, and I found that dreams are where our brains sort out what happened during the day. That made sense, and I rationalized that my nightmares were just caused by my busy day. Without realizing it, my mind chose to block out the notion of ever being assaulted, so it wasn't part of my thinking anymore. I told myself my brain was just working out my work stress, something everyone dealt with. I took a deep breath and began getting ready for work.

Transformative Tip #8

Have you ever thought about grief outside of losing a loved one? The need to grieve is an important process for experiencing all aspects of life—no matter if it's a breakup, the loss of a pet, or the end of a friendship. Take the time to grieve fully. This means experiencing what happened without judging yourself, others, or the circumstances overall. It means simply feeling from your heart without your head adding anything. I didn't pause, journal, or reflect on my emotions from losing my dad and brother. I was focusing all my energy on surviving my life shifts, which meant avoiding my feelings of sadness. Thriving means letting yourself feel your feelings and using the experiences you've had to help you grow. Know that no matter what happens, you can handle it. Embrace your feelings rather than running from them. There's no deadline when it comes to grief. You don't need to return to your daily life and responsibilities until you're ready. Give yourself some grace and kindness.

Maybe what you're feeling seems too hard to handle. Often, emotions can be scary because we're taught that if we feel that deeply we may never be able to move on with our lives. We fear we won't be able to survive feeling the full weight of our painful experiences. The opposite is actually true, the longer you put off dealing and processing something from your past the more it keeps repeating in the future. It may be hard but the only way to heal it is to feel it. If that means stopping and creating a slower life for a while, so be it.

Some moments in life happen not to stop us completely but to encourage us to simply pause and reflect. Share your feelings with someone who can help you better understand your pain and work through all the stages of grief from denial to acceptance and growth. It's ok to take a break and to let what happened sink in. You can choose how you'll live your life in a new powerful way from what you experienced. I promise you're stronger than you could ever possibly know. After all, you are wired to survive.

CHAPTER 9: ACKNOWLEDGING OTHERS

I didn't pay much attention to the news until my friends started talking about something in the mortgage industry that could have an impact on the economy. I had a job, so I didn't pay much attention to what they were talking about until I went into work for our monthly front office leadership meeting. At the meeting, I was informed we'd need to rank all our employees from best to worst performers since twenty-five percent would need to be let go. Life continued to become more and more uncertain. I'd been thinking about applying for the promotion I'd decided on the year before, but it no longer seemed like a smart idea. The news, my mom, and the other leaders at the hotel told me to stay put.

My mind was in a whirlwind, and the thoughts and worries wouldn't stop! Would I lose my job? Would I lose my apartment? A friend of mine moved back in with her mom after losing her brother to suicide and later her job due to the recession. Should I just give up and go home? I tried to find the glass half full. I was grateful to be able to go to the beach more often and have more down time. Soon I was down to working only three days a week, but I was relieved to still have a job. Surprisingly, a recession in Miami meant the bars and clubs were begging for business and would give away an hour or two of free alcohol to get people in the door. I created a Miami Event Listserv in my email to easily share the event invitations with others, and I loved the extra time with my friends. At twenty-six, I was grateful to still be able to feel young and free.

Unfortunately, that feeling didn't last long. I quickly discovered the recession meant we were expected to deliver the same level of customer service to our hotel guests but were left with half the amount of people to take care of them because the hotel terminated most of our hourly employees. I was having a hard time taking even a fifteen-minute lunch break, and my eight-hour schedule morphed into ten-hour days. I could've accepted that some days I'd have to work late and not see my friends, but I didn't want to sacrifice anything. I was in a race to have it all. I became obsessed with doing everything and not missing out on any opportunity.

Working hard was the only way. Downtime was wasted time. I became obsessed with impressing my boss and would live for the times she'd give me special projects because I knew it meant she trusted me. I'd work 3 p.m. to 1 a.m. and then speed home and search the streets of South Beach for good parking. Sometimes this would take thirty minutes to an hour. Often, I'd park and then realize I left my apartment keys at work. After searching my entire car, I'd be forced to drive back downtown to work and once again sit in traffic. I was completely exhausted, but I was going to have a life! I would quickly change, make myself a drink for the road, and meet my friends out at a bar somewhere. By the time I got there, they were already drunk, and I'd have to chug my drinks just to catch up.

I started to resent Miami because I realized I was working almost as hard as if I were in New York City. What do they say? You can take a girl out of New York, but you can't take New York out of the girl. I had grit, determination, and I was willing to work as many hours as needed to get promoted. However, I wasn't acknowledged or appreciated. I knew I deserved more opportunities or a raise.

I became frustrated very quickly because hard work wasn't held at as high of a value in Miami as it was in New York. Since jobs were limited, I felt fearful I wouldn't be able to find anything else. When I asked some of the managers at my hotel for advice, they said if I left the company, I'd have a hard time getting back in again.

Often after working until 1 a.m., I had to be back at 7 a.m. the next day. The rates at the hotel were lowered as fewer people were traveling, and the company was desperate for occupancy no matter how much we had to lower the price to get, as they say, "heads in beds." The type of guests attracted to these prices had little manners. Guests would yell and curse at me on a daily basis. I would ask about training for other positions, but there was always a story for why that was impossible, or they'd tell me it was okay for me to train and then come find me and ask me why I wasn't at my post. The more stressful work became, the more I wanted to be where I felt happy—with my friends. Although I wasn't working that many days a week, I never realized the physical drain of being mentally stretched so thin. I kept thinking of my brother, Richard, and how his focus was never on money or success but on his friends instead. Trying so hard to give a hundred percent to everything, I was burning myself out.

I'd wake up in a panic night after night and fall back to sleep. Often, I'd sleep the morning away only to wake up at 1 or 2 p.m., right before I had to get ready for work. Then I would quickly shower, all the while thinking I was going to be late. Once I was finally ready, I'd realize I had no idea where I'd parked my car the night before or where my keys were. I started to feel the world closing in, and my brain could barely think and focus. The harder I tried to remember where my car was, the more difficult it became. Then I'd hear my boss's voice in my head chastising me for running late. Eventually I'd find my car, promise myself I'd find a better system for remembering where I parked, and repeat the cycle over and over again. I'd immediately dry my tears, put on some energetic music, and drive blindly to work, barely noticing the beautiful view of clear, blue waters, cruise ships, and palm trees around me. I'd give myself a pep talk, turn the door into the hotel, and paste a smile on my face. I kept repeating, "I can handle this," but in reality, I couldn't.

My stomach sank the day I came in for a meeting and Jessica announced we were to have a renovation of the guest rooms. At first, I was happy, the guests had been complaining about the quality of our rooms, and I wanted a hotel of which I felt proud. Then the other shoe dropped. The owners were forbidding us from telling the guests about it before they arrived. There was no mention of it on the website either.

The guests would arrive, and I'd warmly say, "Welcome."

"What's that noise?" they'd ask.

"Oh, we are just having a small renovation."

"What? No one told us!"

That would be my day every day. As the face of the hotel, working the front desk is incredibly difficult even on a good day. Now imagine lying and going against your morals on a regular basis. The airline crew who stayed at our hotel would wake up every day at 7 a.m. and call down, yelling at us about how they might not be able to fly because they didn't have enough sleep. My mind kept exploding, but I believed the empty promise that if I worked hard, I'd move up. I'd go out with my other supervisors after work, and we'd all vent. Realizing I was not alone with this frustration made it a bit easier to cope, but nothing changed, and I felt I was selling myself out every single day.

By the end of 2008, I won the Supervisor of the Year award. I'd managed to turn the rape, one of the worst things to happen to someone, into an immense dedication to my job. I would work whatever hours I could, becoming a sacrificial lamb yearning for approval and to be accepted. Remember those awful, challenging days I mentioned before? This was that kind of day over and over again. My boss, in many ways, created much of the power dynamic I felt during my assault, and when I'd express displeasure at how many hours I was working or the lack of staff we had, she'd never empathize or let me know my voice was heard. If she'd assured me she understood what I was going through, being pulled so thin during this time of economic decline, perhaps I would've felt more appreciated and fulfilled at my job. Instead, I just felt empty and exhausted. She'd point to her assistant manager who was a level above me and remind me she also was doing more than normal, and I shouldn't complain. This answer wasn't really enough for me, but I felt foolish and wrong about sharing my displeasure.

After the assault and losing my brother, I stopped trusting my choices. One night, a woman came in late with a dog, asking if she could check in. My first instinct was to say no because dogs were not allowed, but it was late, most hotels were sold out, and I felt compassion for her. I knew my job was to protect the hotel, so I told her she would need to give a $250 deposit fee, which she agreed to. I went home that night with my head high, feeling something had mentally shifted. Instead of calling my boss at midnight or turning the guest away, I'd found a solution. I had trusted myself!

Imagine my shock and displeasure when I came in the next afternoon, and Jessica immediately asked me to come into her office and close the door. She told me she'd heard I'd allowed a woman with a dog to check-in, and she was very disappointed I'd do that when dogs were not welcome. My face immediately fell, and after that, I'd avoid making decisions at any cost. When someone doesn't feel heard, they stop trying. They avoid engaging, and they go through the learned motions that keep them under the radar. I mentally checked out of my day and put one foot in front of the other, as if in a robotic state. I'd go into work with the sole intention of just getting through another day.

Some days, I'd fleetingly think about the rapid career growth I'd once firmly believed would be a possibility, and I'd scrounge up the courage to brainstorm what I needed to do in order to create a promotion in the future. I would ask Jessica if I could train in food and beverage to get more experience in another department, and she'd say, "Yes." Training day would come and go, and she'd come up with reasons for why I had to be at the front desk instead. I was the one there at 11 p.m. when she was fast asleep. I was the one dealing with unhappy, late guests. Yet, I was never praised or recognized for my empowerment. I was only told not to make the choices I'd made again. I became scared of making a decision or giving the type of quality service I craved to deliver. I started to resent that I was the highest ranked manager in a six hundred room hotel during the evening shift and was never thanked for dealing with all the problems. Instead, I was reprimanded.

The worst of all was combined in two separate days I'll never forget. One day, Jessica, my boss, sent me home because my pants were too tight. I drove home in a mad panic and contemplated not going back, but like a moth to a flame I returned, hoping for her approval. Fear: that's how toxic work environments thrive. People are scared to leave and think they have no worth. Over the four years I was there, I'd ask about moving up constantly. I was always told I wasn't ready, and twice I watched positions above me filled with a manager just out of college. When I asked what I needed to do to move up, they said they wouldn't have time to teach the skills to me.

The second day was in December 2008 at my annual review. My manager said I wasn't managing my time well and needed to cut down on overtime because I was an hourly employee. I tried to explain that there were only two to three of us at the front desk including myself. Most hotels have one per every hundred fifty rooms but we had six hundred rooms, meaning there should have been four or five of us at the desk. Having enough staff would have allowed me to check on our staff in the vip lounge and walk the property to make sure everything was smooth. It would also have allowed me to spend time during my shift dealing with guest issues and complaints. Instead, after I completed my front desk clerk responsibilities, I'd start on my supervisor duties. These tasks consisted of such duties as writing up the notes about guest complaints and staff payroll. Once I finally completed my notes, I was so exhausted and could barely keep my eyes open. I'd try to talk to my coworkers, who were great, but they had no solutions either. I told my boss that I was trying my hardest, but it simply wasn't possible to leave after only eight hours. She replied, "Find a way."

Somehow, even though we were all talented, between the recession and the toxic, disempowering work environment, we all felt frozen and stayed in a position for four years that most people would've moved on from after six months. My "bible," as one of my fellow staff would call it, was a book listing every guest who needed follow-up on their complaint. We'd pass this book on from shift to shift. Most supervisors just threw it together and ran out the door. I cared—my Achilles heel—and stayed to get the job done well.

The day of my review, Jessica handed me a brush and told me I needed to brush my hair. I felt I couldn't win with her, but I couldn't leave a job half done; it just wasn't me. I would write down that I left two hours earlier than I did, out of fear of getting into trouble, noting 11 p.m. everyday instead of 1 a.m., essentially working for free during that time. Money wasn't my priority, though. All I wanted to do was succeed, move up in the company, and of course, make my dad proud.

I was determined to have it all in all areas of my life, and I was out almost every day after work and on my days off at fashion events, new liquor roll-out parties, restaurant openings, free movies, and other social occasions. This may sound exciting, but I was just doing what I trained myself to do. These events were no longer fulfilling or fun. I was just too tired to relax and enjoy. In 2009, the term *fear of missing out* (FOMO) became popular, and my fear felt cemented. Staying home meant I was giving myself permission to give up on that promise to have a great life, which at twenty-nine meant not missing out on anything Miami had to offer. I literally felt more stressed and anxious when I stopped and did nothing than when scheduling a fully packed day. The days I'd sit on the beach and watch the waves only made me feel more alone. I'd listen, searching for answers, but I was only met with my thoughts saying, "You're stuck; you're trapped." I was surrounded by coworkers, friends, and family who loved me, yet it was like I was frozen, and they were at a distance. I could barely feel their love. I just wanted to shake away the dark cloud that followed me, the protective layer keeping me from really feeling. I remember a day when I was getting my car's oil changed. I sat outside and waited. I looked at the palm trees and the beautiful Biscayne Bay, and my voice barely whispered, "It's so beautiful here, why am I so sad?"

I'd get mad at myself for feeling upset believing one should only experience good feelings, like happiness. I wasn't embracing that our feelings are wonderful indicators of what is serving us and what is not. I should've used that sadness to see what I could have done to change my life.

I took all my anger out on my city. I had to blame someone or something, so I blamed Miami. I hated all the choices I'd ever made. It's amazing how the brain works. When you're determined to be miserable, you somehow view even the greatest things as negative and tend to attract them. I stopped being grateful. I'd go to brunch with the same friends almost every Sunday before running to work. We'd repeat similar conversations about dating and jobs; the only difference would be the name of the men and maybe the role at work. Instead of appreciating that I was able to eat outside mid-winter and create strong relationships with my girlfriends, I was angry that the conversations were about our superficial lives. My mind was both mad and sad because I was dealing with the repercussions of the long-lasting trauma from my rape, my nightmares, and my toxic boss. I'd complain that hunting for a parking spot in South Beach was awful or about the exhausting forty-five minutes it took to drive what should be fifteen minutes home on the weekends.

I didn't stop and ask myself what the solutions were to these problems. I could get a job closer to home or move to an apartment with parking spots available. I was so closed off to anything positive that I didn't see what was really possible. I'd post questions on Facebook, like "Where should I move?" or "What cities are best for people in their twenties?" I thought about leaving, but I wanted someone to come with a magic wand and take the giant risk for me. I thought, if I just moved away, my life would be better. I didn't trust myself, so I avoided taking any responsibility for my life.

I felt stuck in the same lifestyle. I forgot what it felt like to be truly alive, present, and thriving. I clung to the constants in my life even though I was secretly miserable. I was barely surviving and contemplated moving back to New York, but I thought I didn't want to be a failure. I didn't want to prove my family right or have those people from high school think I couldn't hack it in Miami.

I was obsessed with the idea of leaving, and I called Miami "the black hole" because of my love/hate relationship with it. Yet, I was in a stalemate. I was still too scared to do anything, and I was in complete denial that every day I was choosing to relive my victim experience. I came to believe that everyone at work was out to get me, and my friends were just using me to organize their social lives. I stopped organizing the meetups even though I loved it so much. I'd wake up every day feeling heavy and exhausted and would battle my way to survive another day in the world.

Transformative Tip #9

Who or what in your life have you stopped appreciating? Begin to actively practice acknowledgment. Acknowledgment is showing true appreciation to another person. How often do you acknowledge the people in your life? How often do you say to your wife or husband that you really appreciate them when they get the kids after school? Or how often do you thank that one friend you can call at any hour of the night? This can be a simple, genuine, personalized, heartfelt thank you: "I just wanted you to know how much I appreciate having you to talk to all the time" or "I know you stayed late yesterday, and it really made a difference. I hope you know how much we appreciate you." The more you help others feel like a million bucks, the more rewarded you feel yourself. We never know what someone else is dealing with, and a kind word or genuine praise can go a long way. Sincere acknowledgment depletes any resentment harbored by people who you may not realize feel taken for granted in your life.

CHAPTER 10: GRATITUDE

In 2010, I finally reached my breaking point at work, when the other two supervisors I was friends with, Ted and Irina, transferred to other hotels. My work support system was now gone, I was training the new supervisors, and *another* renovation was announced. While we were allowed to tell the guests before they came this time, we still had the same limited staff with which we'd been scraping by since 2008. The lobby was being renovated, meaning guests had to be driven via golf cart up to the third floor to check in at reception. We'd have to walk ten minutes from the employee entrance to the front desk with our heavy cash banks in hand. The desk was a makeshift five-foot table with three people crammed behind it. Once again, hotel rates went down, and the treatment from guests got worse.

I kept comparing myself to the other supervisors. I knew I had more guest name mentions and put in more hours than anyone else, so why was I the last one promoted? I recalled the days I'd abandon plans on my day off to replace an associate who called in sick. I'd wonder if it had been worth it. When my counterparts left, I started to see how I'd been fooled. Although my leaders repeatedly told me I wasn't ready to become a manager, I saw the opposite was true. I was more than ready.

The front office and assistant front office managers, Stephanie and Mandy, would take turns taking the weekend off, and I'd get saddled with half of their work and no weekends off to see my friends. They told me as managers they were working twelve to fourteen hours a day, and when I was a manager, I could have more weekends off. I continued to pour my heart into the job and say "yes" to the extra work because I still hoped it would convince Jessica to create an opportunity for me. I trusted blindly and became addicted to validation from the few times she'd say, "Good job." I believed people were good at heart and even though my friends said I should leave, I stayed, hoping and praying my boss would finally see what I'd accomplished. I had invested way too much time and energy to leave with no reward, and I secretly wondered if anyone else would want me. I'd go home and update my resume, but I'd never have the courage to actually press the apply button.

After a while, my stress and exhaustion manifested physically. One day I was with my mom having a salad on Ocean Drive, a street right next to the beach, when I jumped up and ran to the restroom with massive stomach pains. I couldn't understand why this was happening since I'd only eaten a salad. With her encouragement, I went to a specialist who quickly brushed me off after my blood tests came back normal, saying it was just stress. After leaving the doctor, I was completely shocked. I thought he would give me a prescription, and I'd be on my way. Being told it was just stress made me feel like I was making a big deal over nothing. Upon leaving, I felt dizzy and had to sit down.

I called my mom, and she kept saying, "What? Stop crying, I can't understand you."

I gulped for air and told her that the doctor said I was only stressed out.

"Stress?" she asked. "Everyone has stress."

I quickly agreed and then sank to the floor, thinking of other times I'd felt dismissed: the police officer after the rape, my boss when I told her what happened, and once again my boss when I told her of my work frustrations. The fact the doctor didn't ask me any more questions or give me any follow-up steps to improve my health made me feel like I wasn't important or worth his time. The feeling of having little value brought me back to the past few events that had turned my life upside down.

From that point on, whenever I would leave work, I'd be struck by pains that were so bad I'd have to stay in the restroom because I was unable to drive home. I'd sit there and resent the fact that because of my bad stomach I was going to be even later meeting my friends. I worked at a busy hotel; I would just have to put up with the stress. I thought about leaving, but every job has its stresses, right?

The day I found out my favorite supervisors' news that they were transferring to other hotels, I should've been happy for them since they were my friends. Instead, I was bitter. I was mad, overwhelmed, and over not being appreciated. I started to ask myself what I was doing. It was like I didn't even exist. No one listened to my ideas, no one cared, and no one could make this feeling go away. Every year, we had a chance to fill out a survey and give feedback on our associate experience. The week before, Jessica, now the assistant general manager, and Stephanie, the front office manager, ran around asking if we were going to score our department a "ten." They explained to me my review depended partially on these surveys. I showed up to fill out the 2010 survey with a knot in my stomach. I wanted to talk to human resources, but I knew the director was best friends with Jessica, and if I confided in them, they'd most likely tell her. When hourly staff members had spoken to human resources, Jessica no longer saw them as promotable, and I didn't want to take the risk. I sat down in front of the computer and cried. No one noticed. I quickly filled out the survey with high scores, hating myself for not being able to speak up.

Perhaps if someone I confided in paused to truly listen and didn't reply before I had even finished explaining, things would've turned out a lot differently. I felt so empty. I was beyond angry. I was pissed, and more than that, I was deeply hurt. It sprung me into action, and I applied to other jobs in the company.

I didn't get the first opportunity, but the second, which was a small ninety-room hotel, was within walking distance from my house. During the interview, I was focused on clearly communicating my priority to develop. The general manager, David, who interviewed me was very charming, and I liked his energy right away. He couldn't stop smiling. A few days later, I was offered the job, and I decided to take the chance. As soon as I informed Stephanie and Jessica, they tried to talk me out of it.

"Oh, they have bad roof leaks every summer. You don't want to work there. The place is falling apart. You still need more time."

Mandy, though, encouraged me to go, saying every hotel in the company was different, and she believed in me. I should try.

It was 2011, and Barack Obama had been president for two years. I kept thinking about his speeches centered on change. It was indeed time for a change. Mandy was right. I deserved better, and I wouldn't allow Jessica to control me anymore. I'd never felt so angry and excited all at once. It was exhilarating! I could improve my life.

I proudly accepted the offer, bragging to people that I was "taking my talents to South Beach," a reference to when Lebron James joined the Miami Heat. I woke up the next day feeling mentally and physically better. I'd put off making any kind of major decision for years, which was physically weighing on me without me realizing. My shoulders had risen up to my ears due to the constant stress and pressure, and it became so noticeable my friend Ray would constantly push my shoulders down when he'd see me. I spent hours asking friends for suggestions on where to move. I would rely on social media to tell me what career I should take on.

I experienced one of my biggest breakthroughs when I realized not making a decision was essentially a choice to stay stuck. The moment I accepted the job offer, I came back to life because I trusted in myself. I'd created a change that would give me the chance to start a new chapter.

The day of my going-away party, my downtown hotel served pork and coconut—two items I repeatedly mentioned I did not eat. It may seem unimportant, but as a manager, it makes a difference to know what idiosyncrasies make each staff member unique. It makes them feel cared for, listened to, and appreciated. After four years, I couldn't believe they hadn't listened to what I shared at every work event and function. If nothing else, I thought they would have asked around before the party to find out my likes and dislikes. This was just one way I felt like a number rather than an individual staff member who was an important part of the company. I was so grateful that I finally woke up as painful as it was. Sometimes you have to get to that point beyond anger when you're done and can no longer care. It can be the catapult into a new life.

Working at my new hotel, not only as a manager, but as the person in charge of the entire front desk and human resources departments, gave me an awesome feeling of responsibility. I told myself this was my chance. My first day I jumped in with both feet, helping guests with luggage and doing whatever I could to contribute to the success of the hotel. My team was small but mighty, and both the general manager, David, and the operations manager, Steve, were laid back, friendly, and supportive. I was able to walk to work and had the opportunity to grab a mojito on my way home. I had a set schedule, ending at 8 p.m. in the evening—though I would often secretly leave at 7:30 p.m.—and was off on Sunday and Mondays. I loved the first few months. But soon after, a few things happened.

First, since Steve and David had worked together before, they would talk to each other during our leadership meetings and assume I knew all the terms they were throwing around. I didn't understand, and because I still hadn't learned to speak up, I felt resentful and left out. I knew their time was valuable and didn't want to slow them down by interrupting with a ton of questions. When my mom came to visit, standing in the small boutique hotel, she announced she liked the other hotel better. It was just her preference, but as a pleaser, I wanted to make her happy. She was my only living parent, and I knew I had an unknown amount of time left with her. I never told her "no" when she asked if she could visit. She would refer to Miami as her petite escapade (little getaway) and would smile every time she'd come see me. It felt wrong to tell her I was too busy and exhausted from work to spend time with her. Yet, I knew I wasn't fully present. Instead, my thoughts were flying in different directions. I wanted to make everyone I knew proud of me. I forgot to look inward and ask myself if I was at peace and content with my decision or if certain situations worked for me.

After some time, I no longer valued the quiet days, the ones where only a few people were checking into the hotel and where most of the day I had little to do. The days were too dependable, boring even. My brain, after so much trauma, only knew chaos and constant change. I wanted busyness; I needed excitement. While at one point in my life the feelings of trauma were foreign and unnatural, by now, it became my norm. I'd lived in a world of unpredictability for so long, I didn't know how to navigate so much extra downtime, or the feeling of empowerment David and Steve gave me. Because the hotel was properly staffed and I had fewer time-consuming tasks, I was able to leave work on time—a very new experience for me. I had a walking distance commute with no stress of finding a parking spot after a long day. Yet, I still couldn't be happy. It was almost like my mind betrayed me.

Instead of appreciating this new life, my mind craved the darkness. It had become an addiction and something I could depend on. Life couldn't be easy; it had to be stressful, rushed and hard. Hope was scary. Trust was even scarier. Making myself proud seemed unimportant. I wanted to keep moving up, and I wanted to brag to people about my title to impress them. I considered leaving for a larger hotel. I decided I was feeling unfulfilled and not challenged at the smaller one. I had unrealistic expectations that I needed to always be busy, constantly learning or doing something. I never stopped to create small and large goals and check them off or celebrate the small changes I was making to improve the small hotel.

Have you ever had a "grass is always greener" experience? No matter what I had I was unable to appreciate it. Instead, I'd always search for what I no longer had or what someone else had. Everything was going right, and everything was easy. I finally had the life work balance I wanted! Yet, I convinced myself I missed the hustle and bustle and started to think about where I would go next.

The people and location working at the smaller hotel made a difference in my decision to stay there. The restaurant servers would make me a fresh breakfast sandwich with crispy turkey bacon in the morning, and Steve would always joke around with us. My ten-minute walk to work helped me clear my head as I'd walk past the art deco buildings and breathe in the ocean breeze just three blocks away. The safety and relaxed nature almost made me feel out of place because I told myself my whole life that you need to be stressed to win. My old hotel would still email me asking for help in editing guests' letters, even though I no longer worked there. Every time I would see Jessica's name in my inbox, my stomach would start to clench up. I couldn't believe they were still asking me for favors, such as helping write guest letters or with other hotel projects. I was no longer an employee there! My confidence returned, and I chose to ignore her requests. I questioned my lifelong belief that in order to be successful, I needed to be a hard worker. I remembered my sales boss telling me to "work smart, not hard," and I tried to imagine what that would be like and how to execute it.

At this hotel, my friend Leslie would stop by with a giant smile and her new baby, Ava, and we'd talk in the lobby. Another friend, Martha, with her long brown ponytail and straight posture would stop by just to say hi or to drop off an empanada from across the street. The first few months, I felt like the luckiest person in the world, but I had yet to deal with the scars and abuse from my last job. I just stood up and pushed on, thinking if I kept going, it would lead me to happiness.

As the months passed, Jessica, my old manager, kept calling my cell phone while I was at work and leaving messages. Every time I'd hear her voice I'd cringe, yet part of me thought, "Good, she missed me enough to call." I'd remember my team at my old hotel property and their families and our jokes and memories. I'd recall while I had been miserable in many ways, I did care very much about the people who worked there. I admit, I was curious why she kept reaching out. I begrudgingly called back. Part of me didn't understand why she couldn't just let me be. Another part of me wanted to show off my progress, how much responsibility I now had, and how far I'd come. After numerous calls, I quietly excused myself from the front desk, walked around the corner, took a deep breath, and called her back.

The phone barely rang when she answered, "Suzie! How are you?"

She was very friendly and positive, mentioning the great job I'd done when I worked for her. My gut kept crunching into a ball, and the conversation was totally uncomfortable. I kept wondering what she wanted. She told me the front desk manager position, the one I had coveted for four years, was going to be available soon, and she would love for me to come back to the hotel. I told her the minimum amount of time to transfer from my new hotel was a year, and I had only been there six months that November. She continued to ask, and I kept saying, "I can't," because I felt bad leaving David and Steve in the lurch.

After she ended the call, I realized she'd gotten into my mind. What was my next move? Jessica did seem genuinely happy to talk and missed me. She said she knew I'd been doing all of my boss's work all those years and wanted to make it up to me. On the one hand, I loved my walks from work to home and avoiding the stress of having to look for a parking spot. But was it about my happiness or moving up in my career? I remembered hearing my mom say how she would commute over an hour from our hometown to the Bronx for many years for her job, and I was debating driving fifteen minutes. Someone was contacting me for an opportunity, while also offering to make up for all my past pain and frustrations when it came to that hotel. A part of me wanted to be able to brag to others that I was one of the main managers of a six hundred room hotel and that Jessica personally called me to come back after leaving. Whenever anything would go slightly wrong at the boutique hotel, I'd think about how it would've been better if I were at the larger one. For example, when two staff members called out, I had to work a fourteen hour shift because I had no one to call in to replace them. At the other hotel, I had a larger pool of people to offer the shift to in an emergency.

In November of 2011, David gave me the task of purchasing the Christmas decorations for our lobby. I went shopping, but all the while I complained to myself that he didn't mention purchasing Chanukah decorations and that he clearly didn't care or respect my being Jewish. All my experiences were only seen in a negative light. No matter what happened, I could only experience life through a disempowering perspective.

As I drove, I passed my old hotel, and memories of past interactions I didn't think were managed well came rushing back. I grouped David in with my past managers and the feelings of resentment, humiliation, and frustration kept stacking up. I came back from the shopping trip upset and felt as though the need to express myself was exploding inside of me.

Upon returning, I saw David in the lobby, and he asked how the Christmas shopping went. A part of my brain felt like a rubber band was breaking, as if my cells were being pulled apart. What about Chanukah? Why were we always the forgotten ones? I screamed at him and had a full-blown meltdown. I have no idea what words came out of my mouth. I felt like I'd blacked out—my legs were walking and my mouth had words, but I wasn't there. Once again, I was watching myself outside of my body.

Did I know on some level that something was wrong? Of course, I did. Yet, I blamed everyone else instead of taking responsibility. Throughout the years, I'd accuse the city, traffic, my bosses, and even my friends for everything. I'd think about leaving, even applying and interviewing sometimes, but I just couldn't do it. It was like a force field keeping me in the only life I had known for seven years.

My brain kept trying to replay the victim-aggressor role I'd experienced during my trauma. For years, my mind kept attempting to make sense of what happened that terrible night when I was raped. Often, people with trauma and depression want more for themselves yet end up turning the anger inward. I was too mad to give myself a proper opportunity to express my needs. Perhaps I could've asked my boss if he'd set aside time for us to talk, or I could've given myself a deadline for how long I should stay in a job without a promotion. However, at that time, anything that meant movement, growth, or a new possibility was fought by my mind. Change meant the unknown, and my mind had learned to survive by making no sudden movements. I developed a fear for anything out of my norm. I'd even take the same streets home from work each day. Most changes in the past five years had only resulted in my barely functioning, so I had to cling to what I knew. Only then could I get through the day.

I started to see authority figures as people who didn't understand me, people who took advantage and who only cared about themselves. If people acted that way, I knew what to do: *run.* So that day, I ran down the street and fell apart. I wondered *"Is this what it feels like to lose your mind?"* Unfortunately, as quickly as the thought came it went away. I convinced myself I was fine and turned around to l with the disruption I created. When I came back, David asked me to come to his office. I thought he was going to fire me. Instead, David spoke to me kindly and apologized for not including my holiday. He encouraged me to buy a menorah for the lobby. I didn't know how to handle his heartfelt sentiment. It had been so long since I heard something like that, but I still held back on opening up to him. I convinced myself I'd be okay, and my anger was just a one-time occurrence.

Transformative Tip #10

What are you grateful for? How can you better incorporate pausing and feeling grateful into your life? How can gratitude be less fleeting? First of all, being grateful isn't just writing a quick list or saying "I'm thankful for my house" on Thanksgiving. There is a difference between just saying you are thankful or grateful and truly stopping and connecting with that statement, really deeply feeling it. Smartleadershiphut.com (*Grateful vs. thankful: Choose wisely to boost your happiness and success 2019*) states "Grateful is feeling or showing appreciation for something done or received. Thankful is a feeling of pleasure and relief." Both are important to practice. If you practice gratitude, it tends to come back to you as your entire perception shifts. If you're depressed, your brain fights you from feeling this gratitude. It focuses on what's wrong, what you don't have rather than all the love and beauty you are surrounded by. So, start with one small affirmation each day, such as "I'm grateful I got out of bed this morning." Then stop and really feel that statement. Think about what it took to do that, what a new day means. "I'm grateful that it's sunny outside." Notice how you feel the sun; notice the birds outside singing. "I'm thankful for all the food in my fridge." Slowing down allows our brain to feel like we're in control. By noticing all we have to be grateful for, we're actually training it to start looking for the good

Every morning, close your eyes and experience three things you're grateful for. I always picture my niece at age six visiting me in Florida and running as fast as her little legs would carry her, or I imagine that first moment I drove over the Miami Beach causeway and smelled the ocean air. Find your happy place and channel it each day. Even if you're tired or angry, take a few minutes to find something to be grateful for. What's truly amazing is that the moment you focus on gratitude, you stop being upset because you realize how much you have rather than what you're missing.

CHAPTER 11: BE IN THE MOMENT

It was April 2012, and I was officially at the beach hotel for a year. This was important because after a year, a salary manager could transfer to another position or hotel if they chose to. By then, it was evident I had overstayed my welcome living in South Beach. I knew every corner, bar, and restaurant there was. I felt trapped because I could easily walk the width of the city in twenty minutes. I needed to have somewhere different to explore and a new life to experience. I was no longer the naïve, doe-eyed, twenty-one-year-old "getting jiggy with it" in her dad's corvette. I was now almost thirty, and my friends were getting married and having kids.

I felt ready for another chapter but had no idea what I wanted to do next. I would walk home from work feeling heavy because I believed I wasn't making the difference I wanted to for our guests and staff. In reality though, our guest and associate surveys showed my impact was present; it just wasn't as massive or immediate as I had imagined it would be. I still hadn't learned the financials, the one part I had been told for years was missing in order for me to become a general manager. I was living in the same apartment I moved into at twenty-two, which went from feeling like this upgraded renovated palace to a four hundred-square-foot shoebox. Having my own place was no longer enough, I now wanted to have a bedroom with a door that closed and a kitchen big enough to be able to host a dinner party. I desired a quiet home instead of people knocking on my first-floor window to get into the building. The upstairs neighbors would blast music and party until 6 a.m., meaning I barely had any sleep.

I would dream of moving somewhere else that had none of the "negatives" of South Beach. I would visit Leslie and her family in their luxury high rise with a view, and when I would leave, I would break down crying. It was peaceful and calm. I wanted that life. I wanted to feel accomplished and grown up and proud of my life and choices. I started to realize I had a fear of changing my life. I would hate myself because I wasn't taking any action and beat myself up for fearing change.

I wanted new experiences and a better life. Any life except the one I had. It was just too predictable and unfulfilling. My friend said it sounded like I wanted it all, and in my heart, I knew I did. The problem was that I was constantly looking where I wasn't successful, what I didn't have. I never stopped to notice the areas where I was succeeding or what I was grateful for. I always wanted to better myself, so what more could I accomplish? Instead of focusing on maybe two or three goals at a time, I had fifty. There was no way I could accomplish them all right away, but I didn't want to eliminate any or pick and choose. What more could I learn, do, and experience? Happiness isn't having a fancy title or lots of money. It isn't saying if I have "x," then I'd be happy. This is a major issue, especially in your twenties when you're told to go to college, get a job, get married, buy a house, and have kids. It's like we're given a to-do list for our lives. Instead of thinking of what we can do or judging ourselves on our progress toward our goals, we compare ourselves to others. Every moment is spent in comparison. You want to know where everyone else is positioned in life. How they rank in their career, socially, their relationship status, and if they have children, and you check up on these things with social media. You start to wonder, what's wrong with me? Why am I not in the same place as everyone else? Where did I get left behind? What can I do to move ahead in this race called life?

After six years of trying to become a manager, I finally made it. Yet, I wasn't happy nor fulfilled. No one seemed impressed that I was a manager. Not even my mom, who upon starting my career had asked why I went to college to make people keys for a living. Instead, now she asked why I had left my past hotel since in her eyes it was bigger and nicer. My friends and the people I met at networking events viewed being a front desk manager as a low ranked job just checking people in all day and helping store luggage. They didn't understand all that went into managing the front desk and why I worked so hard for such little pay. So, what do you do when you try everything to prove yourself to people, and they don't really respond? You try harder!

I was lost in thought, blindly walking home on Espanola Way, one of my favorite streets in South Beach. As I wandered, I barely noticed the European style buildings with the balconies above. I passed the mojito bar with thirty different kinds of mojitos. I walked by the French crepe restaurant with the smell of Nutella wafting out. All I saw was failure. All I heard was, "You haven't made it."

That's when it happened. My phone rang. I looked down, and my stomach tightened with fear and anxiety. On the display the name said,

"Old hotel-work." I debated answering, but I felt bad not picking up, and just like every other time they called, I hoped somehow they were calling to acknowledge me.

Jessica spoke very quickly. Again, the front desk manager position was available, the one I had coveted for years. I had left them a year ago and was now eligible to transfer. She said she really valued and appreciated me and knew I could be the one to make the difference. As she spoke, without warning I leaned against a wall and tears rolled down my face. Jessica was saying everything I ever prayed to hear. I wasn't sure if I could trust her, though, because I heard a lot of this before, so at first, I said, "No."

Yet, for some reason, I stayed on the phone. A big part of me said to run, but her words were like a drug, and I was drawn in. Even her voice somehow had power over me. In my heart, since that first day at the job fair when I was feeling lost after my dad and she believed in me, I felt indebted. After all, who else was approaching me, offering the next step in my career?

In my heart I knew it was time to leave Miami, but maybe if I did this job for a year, I could find a better position when I transferred. I was totally lost in thought, internally debating what I should do and say. I barely heard what she was saying anymore. I got silent and felt a release of tears and pain. As I walked, I realized how much I enjoyed my laid-back meandering, rather than the thirty to forty-five-minute traffic and crazy search for parking when I worked downtown.

Jessica kept saying what a great opportunity it was—huge for my career—and that she would personally adopt and take care of me. The more she talked, the more I thought maybe this was worth a shot. She then invited me to have lunch with her at the hotel to discuss further. As I closed the car door and buckled my seatbelt to meet her, I kept saying to myself that I shouldn't go.

As I drove, I found myself caught in contradicting thoughts. One part of me was thinking, "She likes you. Go. It's a bigger hotel, more impressive. Go." The other was thinking, "Are you crazy? Don't go back there!" It is truly maddening when you argue with yourself. I have to admit part of me wanted to go just to show her how much better I was doing without her. Have you ever wanted to prove you were doing really well to someone else? Somehow other people's doubts can spur you forward.

As we chatted outside by the water, I barely noticed the beautiful greens and blues of the islands, Miami Beach, and the causeway. I didn't feel the soft, gentle breeze. Instead, I realized how much happier I was not to be working at this hotel—my old hotel—anymore. Memories of what my days used to feel like, defeated and exhausted, caused me to realize this wasn't what I wanted to experience again. Jessica was relentless, she told me she wanted to make it up to me. She shared with me she knew my bosses often delegated their work to me. She knew I deserved a promotion years ago. She convinced me that the hotel was better now. There were no more renovations, and they had a bigger budget for staffing. As a manager, I would have more control over my schedule.

She had many strong points, but I couldn't get rid of the pit in my stomach, and I told her "no" again. At that point, we finished eating, and she asked if I wanted to stop by and see my old team. She knew my weakness, the hourly front office staff and the entry line crew who barely made any money but carried the hotel on their shoulders. She took me to the back office of the front desk, where the desk agents, bellmen, and phone operators were working diligently. I still wasn't convinced.

Then I locked eyes with Nicole, who would be my direct boss. She had on glasses and looked exhausted, and my heart went out to her. When we made eye contact, I saw myself in her. She really needed help. My old staff then clustered around me and said how much they missed me, how much I mattered, and how they hoped I would come back. That was it. How could I say no? I was needed. I accepted her offer to interview and was given the job soon after.

Transformative Tip #11

Do you struggle with being fully present? Being in the moment? If mentally you are stuck in your past or future, you're not here in the present. This is where the magic happens. Naturally our brains like to wander, so make yourself aware, and catch yourself when you're rehashing the past or analyzing the future. This takes time and is a muscle we must build, so try with three minutes of only thinking about the past or future, then five, then eight. In time, this will become easier. Accept the past, and let it go—no matter what happened. It's good enough to reflect on it afterward and write down what you learned. However, don't spend too much time thinking about what you wish you'd done. It won't change your present, and you'll only torture yourself. Instead, use these lessons to create the kind of future you want, and discover what is truly important to you. I regret I spent most of my energy focusing on my career years ago. I could spend my time rethinking about those years and my choices. Instead, I make better decisions today, now that I know better. I use my past to catapult me to a better future.

The harder you are on yourself, and the more you try to control the future, the less you're enjoying the present moment. After all, isn't life just a series of moments and experiences? When I was a kid, I used to celebrate my half birthdays. My mom would always tell me not to rush my life away, and she was right. When I was twenty-one, I wanted to be thirty and established. When I was thirty, I wanted to be thirty-five and settled down and married. Be where you are. I love that children have no interest in yesterday or tomorrow. Learn from them! They are all about living in the now. It takes some work to be in the moment, but it's definitely worth it to feel alive. You can practice being present in a few ways, such as meditating as well as catching yourself when you're speaking with friends and you're obsessing about the past or future.

CHAPTER 12: LISTEN TO YOUR GUT

Going back to the downtown hotel meant saying goodbye to the random friends wandering by my hotel and popping in to say hello. One friend in particular, Martha, whom I had grown closer to that past year because she lived within walking distance and also worked a non-traditional schedule, would be harder to see once I changed jobs.

We had a tradition that I looked forward to every week. We would grab snacks together every Wednesday. That bit of consistency meant the world to me. Martha would meet me at the South Beach hotel, and we would catch up and walk to the New World Symphony outdoor space to watch free movies. Having a professional orchestra in a beautiful new performance space was a symbol to me of how the city was changing. When I first moved, Miami still had a small-town feel. As the years went by and high rises and cultural opportunities sprung up it started to feel more and more like a big city. By 2012, my friends were not only hanging out in South Beach but also areas like Wynwood, Brickell, and the Upper Eastside.

There was a feeling in the air that whispered, "This won't last forever. It's time to go." As I approached my thirtieth birthday, the nights became extra special to me because I knew I was changing as well. My friends were moving to other cities with more job opportunities, checking out other social groups, and getting married. My twenties were almost over and drinking and going out to the clubs to bring some random guy home felt empty.

Although she was a little older, Martha made me feel understood. She was a calm, quiet beauty, wearing very little makeup with her hair up in a ponytail. She would join me on adventures anywhere from eating on Lincoln Road to going for a drive. Her calm energy was one of acceptance, and her laughter filled my soul. Martha's apartment was half the size of mine, but the pride she had in having her own place after a divorce and moving cities was not to be missed. She was trying to figure out her life, and we would sit together, share a piece of cake, and talk for hours. She lived six blocks from me, and we would walk home from our shared snack and lunches together. One evening while walking home from dinner, I was telling her about how I missed my brother, Richard, and she said in a quiet voice, almost a whisper, "I miss mine, too."

I was confused since I had met her older brother months before. She must've seen the look on my face because she added, "I had another brother, look it up."

My face went into shock and my heartbeat sped up when I noticed she'd used the past tense. She could clearly sense my discomfort, but before I could ask any questions, she merely told me to Google it and turned and walked away. I Googled her last name and brother to find out he'd been kidnapped and murdered as a young boy. My heart went out to her, but I didn't know how to put my feelings into words. I felt my chest tighten and experienced a deep pain as if someone was stabbing me in the stomach. Why did bad things happen to good people? I just didn't understand how my amazing, kind friend had survived something so awful. I was unable to read something so horrible when I had yet to process my own tragic events. I didn't know what to say or how to bring up the conversation about what I'd read.

A million thoughts went through my head. How had I missed such a big thing? She seemed so happy-go-lucky. What else did I not know? Looking back on that day, I wish I had said something to her in the days afterward, anything but pretending that the exchange hadn't taken place. We never talked about that conversation or her younger brother again.

Being in the moment and savoring my memories was my focus at the end of my twenties. When I went back to working downtown, this became a struggle. At first it was great. I will always remember my first day back at the hotel. I walked in, and three of our staff were in the lobby just to greet people and welcome them to the hotel. We had doubled our staff! I could finally breathe and didn't mind that I was now required to work a ten-hour day. I was a manager in a recently renovated, large hotel. Then a few months went by, and it was no longer summer. Fall and winter meant the busy season in Miami. Typically, in Florida hotels, higher occupancy months had more hours set aside for the staff. However, this year, we had the same number of hours budgeted no matter the month. We doubled in hotel occupancy, so twice the number of requests and double the lines at check-in. All the extra staff seen in the lobby months ago were now running around doing tasks, and suddenly, it felt as if we didn't have enough help once again. My ten-hour days had transformed into twelve.

One day, when I was feeling angry, I knocked on Jessica's door and asked if we could talk. I explained my frustration because I was barely able to take care of the guests, yet I was expected to survive extended shifts while being under the pressure to deliver excellent guest satisfaction scores! Many days I would try to take a break just for an upset guest to come to the front desk and demand to speak to the manager, cutting my break short.

Her explanation was that the last manager hadn't budgeted correctly, and now we had no money left for the end of the year—no solution, just "this is how it is." It was like no one was hearing what I had just proclaimed.

That same day, I met Martha at Icebox, our favorite cafe with huge cake slices. Just as I was about to vent, she told me she'd quit her job. She couldn't deal with the toxic environment and abuse from her boss any longer. She kept saying how her boss talked down to her and didn't trust her. I was so shocked that this sweet, easy-going girl would quit her job. I felt her pain.

Martha asked if I knew anyone hiring in the hospitality field, and I panicked. I had to somehow help her, but I felt overwhelmed by the responsibility of trying to find her a job in a field I wasn't sure I wanted to be in anymore. I was exhausted trying to keep myself going and getting to work each day, the idea of helping someone else felt like an obligation rather than an opportunity. I told her I'd ask, but there was a certain distance in the conversation. I think she sensed the annoyed, stressed energy I was giving off even though I tried to hide my upsetting interaction with my boss. Having to help anyone beyond my staff and hotel guests was just too much. Later that day, she emailed me apologizing for asking and that she didn't mean to make me uncomfortable. The crazy thing is she hadn't. She actually showed me what I'd been dealing with wasn't okay. Helping people was my passion, and here I was resenting her for casually asking me for help. As had become my new normal, I mentally checked out. It was all too much, and I never emailed her back. I didn't know how to say that I was dealing with similar abuse at work, so I ignored it.

The days went by very rapidly in a sea of long hours, staff frustrations, guest complaints, and searching for parking spots. I had overstayed my welcome in Miami; what was glamorous years ago was now just a regular day in the neighborhood. Instead of going to the beach daily, I would end up only going once a month. My friends stuck to their own neighborhoods, and even though I would email my schedule weekly to them, they had less patience for all my last-minute changes. What was exciting to me at twenty-two years old—having a schedule where I could sleep until noon and every week bringing a different day—was annoying at twenty-nine. Mostly, I wanted to feel progress in my life.

Jessica would still pop into my office just as I was about to leave, asking for help with one more thing. Nicole, my direct boss, and I got along well, but she would want to "take care" of the supervisors who were at the level below me first, giving them most weekends off, leaving me alone and frustrated. I would try to finish up at the end of the night, wanting so badly to meet my friends, but instead I'd come home and collapse. I told myself I'd deal with this for a year and then transfer, but once it got closer to the year mark, I made a mistake out of exhaustion, and they wrote me a written warning for my file, which meant I couldn't apply for another job for six months.

I was told I needed to keep a better eye when handling cash payments, but I was having an extremely hard time focusing and remembering simple tasks. All my life, I had run into tasks that didn't come naturally to me. I knew if I worked hard enough I'd find a way to get better. I created different systems, using excel or a piece of paper to keep track of my count, and nothing worked. I told myself I was just tired, and eventually I'd get better at handling money. I didn't want to be weak and kept trying even harder. After a while, I accepted it was something I wasn't good at and would ask the staff to help me count my drawer. Then, the upper management team added a gift shop to the mix, so we had two cash deposits each evening. I was trying to make sure rooms were clean at night, monitoring all staff breaks, restocking the front desk, and everything else under the sun. By then it was midnight. After another long evening with very little food or water, I finally started to count my bank and do my shift notes only to nod off midway and wake up startled. I knew it was all too much, but I had given up on trying to communicate to my management team.

I thought about going to human resources, but I felt this would be disloyal to Nicole and Jessica. Most days before work, I'd see Martha knock on my window and surprise me, encouraging me to go for a beach walk or just say hello. At first, I'd hide because I didn't have energy to put on a happy face, but after a few minutes I knew I missed her and would open the door. The nightmares wouldn't end and after years of having them, they became normal. I'd wake up and be happy and thankful they weren't real, and I'd wait for my breathing to slow down and allow air in, all the while telling myself it was just a dream.

After some time, Martha was one of the few friends I got together with. She still wasn't working and even though we would talk less and less each time, being lost in our own thoughts, we still insisted on being with each other. Even in silence, we were a comfort to one another. She became thinner and paler, and I knew something was wrong. I felt a dark energy in the space between us. It was as if Ursula, the Sea Witch from *The Little Mermaid*, had stolen my voice. It was truly the most awful feeling to see my friend suffering and know I couldn't do anything to help her. So, in my soul I prayed. I told myself she would be okay and find a new job soon. She asked me one time in a cryptic text message for fifty dollars, and I gave it to her without question. I'd keep inviting her out, but she often didn't respond, and when she did, she had a reason she couldn't join me. She would text me stories about people out to get her. She wasn't making much sense, and I felt a little afraid and uncomfortable. I couldn't take any more in; my life was heavy enough. I knew she was a smart, strong girl and would sort it out. At times I would invite her out of obligation, but I hoped she wouldn't join us because I felt guilty smiling and laughing when she was stone faced, quiet, and serious.

As the end of 2012 drew closer, I accepted that my social life barely included her. I trusted her to sort out whatever she was dealing with. Therefore, I was in shock when, in mid-October, I received a text from her asking to meet up. It had been a long time, and I was happy to see her reaching out. She accepted my invitation to join a few other friends and me at a restaurant in downtown Miami. During the entire ride, though, we drove in complete silence highlighted by the radio blaring party songs. I asked in my heart and mind, "What's wrong?" but the words never came out of my mouth. I just didn't have the energy for someone else's troubles. I could only focus on keeping myself going. I was drowning, yet no one could tell.

One day in December, as I was walking on Lincoln Road, I saw Martha's dad and brother eating at a nearby restaurant. My gut told me to talk to them, but I remembered Martha told me she didn't trust them anymore. She was mad at her dad and was upset her brother kept siding with him. I didn't want to make her mad by going behind her back. I walked a few steps toward home, looked back at them, looked to the sky toward heaven, and decided to keep walking. It wasn't my place.

On December twenty-first, Martha came over with an empanada and a turtle pendant that said "lucky." My eyes were facing down, and I was having a hard time making eye contact because I felt like a truck had run me over after working so hard the night before. In a flat, lifeless voice she announced that she'd decided to move to Atlanta, where she'd lived previously. It should've been a celebration of a new start, but something just didn't feel right. It sounded more like it was the only option left. I told myself I knew when I went back to visit my college friends I always felt better, so maybe going back to the friends she'd known for many years was actually a good thing.

A few days later, she asked me to stop by before she left. I procrastinated. The idea kept me feeling anxious, and when I walked outside, I felt like I couldn't breathe. I told myself, "Today is about her, not your feelings."

I stopped by CVS, got her a goodbye card, and walked the stairs up to her tiny apartment to help her pack. We took a break, and she got me a mango smoothie from McDonalds. It was something small, but it reminded me of the kind of person and friend I'd been lucky to meet in such a strange city. She walked me to my car, and I called work to tell them I'd be late, which was immediately met with a reprimand about being on time. We embraced to say goodbye, but it was like hugging a ghost. I felt only space and distance and all we had not said. I noticed she was just a skeleton with blankness where her eyes used to light up with a witty comment or joke. I drove away looking back at her, not being able to ignore the feeling in my stomach. It was the exact same one I had felt the last time I saw my brother alive.

I told myself this was different. She would be with friends and family soon. That night, I saw a few of her friends I'd met when they visited from Atlanta on Facebook Messenger, but I figured they would know how to help her and signed off. A few days went by, and on December twenty-ninth I called her. I was greatly surprised when she answered. Her voice was so tiny that I strained to hear it. We talked for a few minutes with some awkwardness, and I told her the same thing I said every time we said goodbye those last few months: "I love you." The only words I knew to say that represented all the millions of words I wished I could share.

On January first, Martha's brother reached out to me. He told me she shot herself in her best friend's apartment a few days after seeing family for Christmas. Before he could finish the sentence, I squeezed my eyes shut and grabbed tightly to my seat. In every cell of my body, I knew. In a state of shock, I prepared a beachfront memorial and informed all our friends. At the memorial, we each wrote a letter and put it in a bottle for her. When I spoke, I felt my heart breaking as I saw the birds flying overhead and pictured all the faces of the crazy, fun, memorable nights of the past seven years. I kept dropping the letters and soon after collapsed on the sand. Planning the memorial took all the energy I had. I dragged myself home crying hysterically, wondering why bad things kept happening.

Transformative Tip #12

Did you know your gut is called your second brain? Growing up, we're taught to use our brain or to listen to our heart, but we don't hear much about our gut. Our gut feeling is our internal compass that helps with how we react to situations. Your gut, your instinct, never lies to you; it is your go-to. When you feel that twinge inside like I felt when I saw Martha for the last time, listen to it! Learn to tune in to your body. It may save your life. For example, if you meet someone at a party and something doesn't feel right, know that it's not in your head but in your gut. If you're deciding on a job, don't ask other people, ask your gut. You will figure out what to do.

Often, your brain tries to find a reason for something, and your heart starts to feel emotion, but your gut knows the way. It has all the answers. Just close your eyes, go somewhere quiet, and listen. The answer will be clear. If you don't hear anything, which once happened to me, I recommend seeing a therapist immediately. A broken gut is nothing to mess with. It means something is blocking you from trusting yourself, and if you can't trust you, who can you trust?

Don't forget to be aware of the rest of your body as well. Often your body feels what's hidden away in your brain. My stomach aches, inability to focus, raised shoulders, my jaw that cracked loudly when I tried to close it, and constant headaches were a sign that something was wrong mentally and emotionally. Falling into a heavy sleep at the beach midday was my body's way of telling me something needed my attention. I would google my symptoms and find some justification for why I was feeling that way and not change anything about my lifestyle. If you're in pain, you may go to a doctor, and they may find nothing physically wrong, which is frustrating. Take a moment to give yourself some self-care, take a day off from work, look at what is stressing you in your life, cancel plans, and stay home for the night. Let your mind heal you by taking care of yourself not just physically but mentally and emotionally as well.

CHAPTER 13: YOU ARE THE ONE

Living on Miami Beach wasn't the same after losing Martha; it got a little colder, a little smaller. When I first moved in 2005, South Beach was the place to be, and my friends from various other neighborhoods would drive to experience the area locals referred to as "The Beach". Multiple other friends lived within walking distance. By 2013, South Beach was mainly a tourist destination with locals going to newer, hipper neighborhoods. Many of my friends who lived nearby had gotten married, had kids, and moved to other cities and states. It just wasn't home anymore. Without my friends reminding me who I really was, checking in on me, and meeting up with me every day off, I was forced to spend more time alone. My friends had served as a welcome distraction when I needed an escape the most. Now, those who were still living in the city were exploring new interests with various friend groups. I was focused on finding a way to relax, to calm my noisy mind. I tried riding a bike, going to yoga in the park, and taking walks, yet nothing seemed to help.

I went into autopilot and became numb to everything around me. I went to work, got through the day, and went home. I would drive over the causeway and mentally check out, hoping the pain would go away. At the start of each day, I'd tell myself I was getting out of work on time to see my one or two younger friends who still wanted to start their night at midnight. I knew this would mean leaving on time as most of my friends didn't stay out late anymore, yet I knew it was highly unlikely. I needed some reward to look forward to—a reason to get out of bed each day—and going out after work was what kept me going. I convinced myself I was fine, that I just had to get through the year and transfer like I said many times before, but I was lying to myself. I pulled away from the old friends who'd reach out from time to time, telling them I had to work late when they would invite me to events. Each time, I would feel my heart sinking as I buried myself at work, now working twelve to fourteen hours a day. It was tough to concentrate, and I feared the outside world. I kept getting into trouble at work and felt hopeless and desperate. This was not how my Miami chapter was supposed to work out.

I knew I couldn't live this way much longer, and just like I had with my dad and brother, I thought about what Martha would've wanted me to do. I slowly picked up the phone, called my insurance, and asked for local therapist recommendations.

One woman was on Lincoln Road, just a few blocks away. Walking there, I already felt better. I was finally taking action to focus on myself and my needs. Just like the lion in the *Wizard of Oz*, I kept repeating to myself, "Courage, I can do this." Maybe these feelings could all go away. I felt like a giant cloud was above me but felt a strong hand pushing me forward. I had no idea what to expect, but I knew I needed to feel better.

I came in and saw the therapist. She was an older woman about sixty years of age. She had me sit down, and once she started asking me about my past, everything spilled out. I couldn't stop talking! Finally, I paused, my heart still pounding.

She then replied, "I'm sorry. Right now, I don't think I can help you."

My fear for years when friends mentioned therapy was that I was beyond help. This fear was becoming a reality. She mentioned something about maybe being able to give me her colleagues' names, but I had already checked out. The idea of having to tell that story all over again was too much.

Once again, my words were not important enough. Once again, I was dismissed. I thanked her and then ran outside, found the nearest wall, sunk down, pulled my knees to the rest of my body, laid my head down, and let the tears I could no longer stop flow out of me. I worked myself up so much I could hardly breathe. People walked by asking if I was okay or needed help. So as not to cause too much of a scene, I finally took a breath, looked at the sky, and tried to loosen my locked muscles. I wrote off ever going to therapy again because, clearly, I was just damaged goods and cursed from the start. I went back to work the next day, hoping to bury my pain.

By July 4, 2013, I felt a little bit better. I began to heal from losing Martha and was missing my friends terribly. I was always really into holidays, and this time, my manager added a supervisor on the shift, so I could try to leave on time. I woke up determined that I could finish working and manage to see my friends afterward.

Out of nowhere, the day became busy because staff were calling out of their shifts, and we had last minute reservations. The supervisor spent the shift in the lobby chatting with guests while I sweated it out both in the back with the phone staff, and at the desk checking people in. I worked right through my meal break, all the while keeping my eye on the prize. Then, a fire alarm was pulled, and the entire hotel had to empty out and wait for the fire department to clear us to go back in. No matter how hard I tried, something always happened. I felt like I was suffocating and went by the water to cry. I was so mad and overcome by my thoughts and emotions.

All I wanted to do was leave on time to see my friends. Was that too much to ask? By the time I got out it was 10 p.m. Once again, I spent thirty minutes stuck in the restroom with my stomach hurting and crying. I would repeat Dave's name because it reminded me of being taken care of and feeling cared about. That night, I drove like a mad woman over the causeway from Miami to Miami Beach. I even tried to get home sooner by taking the further causeway that typically had less traffic. Halfway through my drive, I hit a gridlock, and I gave up. I pulled over to the side of the road, and watched the fireworks alone from my car, feeling defeated. I breathed in the view of my beautiful city, and my only thought was, "Why is this so hard?" By the time I drove toward my apartment and parked, I assumed my friends were already home as the firework show was over. I didn't even text them to ask. I was upset and disappointed in the world. My eyes felt like they were a hundred pounds, and my body felt so weak. I went to bed and woke up to texts at 1 a.m. asking where I was and what happened to me. I kicked myself for not reaching out to them. The thought of knowing they were only a few blocks away and I missed out was painful.

It was my thirty-first birthday in August of that year. As I sat with my friends, we joked and told stories of my past birthdays. I realized the only constant force in my life for the past eight years had been my friends. With every week-long birthday celebration, my friends were there for me. They were there for every crazy random night out. Every time I needed an escape, adventure, or simple connection, they were there.

I talked to my mom about my troubles at work, and she said, "Sue, you give and care too much. Work is just something you do so you can afford to enjoy the other parts of your life."

This upset me because I was born in the have-it-all generation. Why shouldn't we have jobs we love? Why shouldn't we care and want to contribute?

I'd go to the hotel every day giving 150 percent, but after experiencing another night crying over the many notes I had to type up in regard to guest complaints, spending an hour counting and recounting my money, not eating for hours, and running to the bathroom in pain after work, I had to ask myself, "Is this worth it?" Is this really what my dad would've wanted for me? What was it costing for me to try to move up and impress people? What, and more importantly, *who* really mattered in my life?

The next day, I went to Mango's, a lounge on Ocean Drive. As I walked up to it, I passed the hotel where I'd hosted my thirtieth birthday only a year before. I remembered thinking no one would come out, as it was in the middle of a hurricane, similar to my first birthday in Miami many years ago. Twenty of my friends and family showed up that day. The birthday storm was truly a symbol for the past decade for me. My friends were my beacons of hope to see me through. At the party, there was a book for people to sign and leave me birthday messages. Martha had written, "Keep your zest for life always."

Thinking about this, I smiled, decided to follow her advice, and met my friend with a new level of excitement at the lounge. I was determined to have a good time to make Martha proud. They played all kinds of Latin music while dancers in leopard print clothes would twirl all over the place. A guy approached me, put out his hand to dance, and I decided, "Why not?" We danced, and I found out even though he had a British accent, he was actually from Brazil and his name was Rodrigo.

Rodrigo and I wound up spending hours walking around South Beach talking, and we proceeded to spend the next two weeks together. I showed him around Miami, and we'd do simple things like watch a movie on my couch with pints of ice cream. It was just the pick-me-up I needed.

There was something about him. For the first time in a long time, I felt total acceptance. He didn't care what club I could get him into or what free event I knew about. He just liked me. For the first time I realized maybe I was enough. The dancer with energy but not the greatest rhythm; the girl who tried her best but didn't always leave work on time; the sophisticated girl who could dress up but secretly was a dork inside. He saw my heart, valued my authentic nature, and that was enough for him. To be that immediately cared for, appreciated, and wanted not solely for physical enjoyment but to be respected as someone you could watch TV and have snacks with meant a lot to me. I had a breakthrough. Maybe I could have a relationship with a guy beyond just a one-night interaction.

We truly focused on getting to know each other, and although my heart had closed up in many ways from my past pains, it had found a way to feel again. On one of my days off, we went to the beach. While we were in the water, his backpack was stolen with most of his extra cash, credit cards, and clothes. Instead of turning against each other, we only bonded more. We walked to my house and found a T-shirt for him to borrow because he was only in his Speedo. We then went to the internet cafe to try to cancel his credit cards and other items that needed to be replaced and reported.

I was finally allowing myself to be in the moment and forget the world, focusing only on Rodrigo and myself being young and having fun. I developed feelings for him, and the affection and support I received brought me to work with a smile on my face. After one week, I asked if he wanted to stay with me, instead of at his hostel. He agreed and one of the last days we were hanging out, I was supposed to leave work at 6 p.m. and was still there at 8 p.m. I knew he was waiting for me at my house, and I felt really bad, plus I was excited to see him. I knew if I stayed any longer, someone would ask me for something else, so I told myself I would double check the total cash my hotel bank had the next day. I was so tired of choosing my work responsibilities over what brought me joy in my life.

The next day, I walked in and saw my boss with a somber face asking me to come right into her office. One of the front desk agents found a hundred-dollar bill stuck to the back of the bank till folded into a small piece of paper. They audited all the banks and found out it was from mine. I felt the blood rush out of my face, but as I had been on the hot seat before and still kept my job, I assumed there was a plan to get me out of trouble. My boss, Nicole, told me she was going to fight it because she knew what a great worker I was. She tried her hardest, but the director of finance said they had given me too many passes. After eight loyal years, many of which I hadn't even claimed my hours, where I worked even though I had a high fever, where I never took a lunch break, where I often came in on my day off, were over. I had too many chances and they had to let me go. No one ever thought to ask me if I was okay or ask how I was doing outside of work.

One lesson I learned as a manager is that often when a good employee's performance starts to decline, there is something going on in his/her personal life. If she can receive the support to deal with whatever is going on, she will often go back to being your biggest asset in time. I truly thought this conversation would be like all the other times when my heart and dedicated work ethic would trump all. Sadly, this wasn't the case.

The moment my general manager told me they decided to fire me, I responded in the smallest, most quiet voice possible. I slowly got out the words, "But this is all I have." At that moment, I truly meant it. Moving up in my career had become an obsession and a way of coping with my dad and dealing with everything else along the way. It was the only part of my life I thought I could control. That same afternoon was my friends' wedding, and I drove there in a fog. As soon as I saw my first friend, I collapsed and fell into their embrace. Everyone gathered around me, asking what happened. I kept repeating, "I lost my job. I lost my job. I lost my job."

My friends hugged me and tried to make me feel better, telling me I worked too much anyway. I didn't want to ruin my friends' wedding, so again I put my tears aside and tried to enjoy the party.

The next day, I went to pick up my items from the hotel in a brown box, and as I drove home, it all hit me. The company I had given so much to and my dream of being a general manager was gone. I looked out and remembered the innocent excitement I had on this same drive just eight years ago. I was no longer that same person. I couldn't try to make this work anymore. It was a sign! I sped to my apartment, started throwing items around, and decided I needed to get out of there. I was moving! It was like my mind and body became possessed. In less than a month, I notified my mom, all my friends, my landlord, and I rapidly sold all my furniture.

My friends asked, "Are you going to look for a new job on the beach?"

"Nope."

"Are you moving to Fort Lauderdale?"

"Nope."

I didn't know what my plan was beyond getting out of there. Away from all the bad memories, the dashed hopes, broken dreams, and trusting the wrong people. I knew—I just knew—I needed to get to my mom's. I painfully found my turtles a new home, said goodbye to them, and had one last brunch with my friends.

Transformative Tip #13

Have you ever waited for someone who would come rescue you from your problems? Well, spoiler: the only one responsible for your life is you. Imagine if I'd realized that five or ten years ago. Work life would've been so different if I'd realized that instead of staying in my job, hoping to be promoted, I had the power to leave. My boss wasn't responsible for waking me up every day and choosing to drive to my job. I was. Once you take full responsibility, you take back your life. We often don't take responsibility because it seems like the more difficult path. It's easier to blame others and wash our hands of what's going on, but that's not a powerful way to live. Your choices are just that—your choices. They don't mean anything about you. You are not a screw up. Often, we're scared to own our lives because we don't want to fail, but owning our choices is the only way to fly.

Please remember that blaming and judging others only takes your power away. We're all human and doing the best we can. You may not agree with how someone handles a situation, and you may not understand their viewpoint, but the longer you hold resentment, the harder it is for you to move on to the greater things in life. Not every decision you make will be perfect. Learn, and let go. Forgive yourself for times you didn't make the right choice and learn from it. Forgive people who hurt you knowing they only did what they felt was the best at the time. This takes time, and I know it can be hard, but you have to let it go.

CHAPTER 14: LIVE WITH INTENTION

Once I arrived at my mom's house, in a quiet retirement community about an hour north of Miami, I breathed a sigh of relief. I had gotten out. As the days went on and I had time to think, the only thing that came to mind was I had to find something positive about this situation.

It's amazing how at five or six years old, we create ways to cope with pain that becomes our default for the rest of our lives. Some people choose to become realists; some choose to expect the worst out of life. I, on the other hand, asked myself where the good was in all of this. Like in any other bad circumstance, the biggest emotion I felt was lack of control. I had to find a way to get my control back. I thought about where I had felt powerful in the past few years, and one word came to mind: traveling. When you travel, any obstacle can be thrown at you, but you know there is always a solution. Once you solve the problem you are rewarded with a certain sense of accomplishment.

When else will I have the opportunity to travel with no end date? Where do I go?

Facebook Status: "Where in the world should I visit?"

Of course, I received about fifty different answers. I tediously wrote them all down and started researching, but I never checked in with myself on where I wanted to go. It was as if who I was and what I wanted didn't matter. I was on this mission to cheer myself up, and I convinced myself that traveling was the way to do it. I found a company that set up trips all over the world. I then gave them my list of destinations for the next five months: Spain, Portugal, Vietnam, Cambodia, Laos, Bali, Singapore, Thailand, Sydney, Melbourne, New Zealand, Fiji, Peru, Chile, Argentina, and Brazil. They designed a ticket that would cost me my entire savings. When they gave me the price quote, my gut tightened, my heart began to beat at a rapid rate, and part of my brain said, "Let's stop and think," but the other part said, "Just go. Show those hotel people how much better your life is now. Live your life and be young."

I felt faint and lightheaded and everything started to spin, but I found myself giving the agent on the phone my credit card number. Everyone was so excited for me, but something felt wrong. I was on a runaway train, and I couldn't get off. My mom and I shopped for a backpack, and I threw myself a bon voyage party. My friends each filled out a colored index card with their name and a personal note including their addresses, so I could send postcards. I created a travel blog to share my experience, and I took off on my journey.

In Spain, I met up with my New York college friend, Miriam, who decided to do a trip for her birthday. We stayed with Elisabeth, an old Miami friend, who now lived in Sevilla. Upon arriving at her apartment, the colored notecards from my friends got wet, and I flipped out, screaming and crying. Miriam and Elisabeth just stood there in shock helping me dry the cards and telling me it would all be okay. I was really starting to spiral inside. After leaving Spain, my friends went back home, and I was on my own.

I went to Portugal next and loved it. While walking to see a castle in Sintra, I randomly met three young travelers from New York, and we celebrated Thanksgiving together. I fell in love with the people, food, and the holiday markets in Portugal and wanted to stay, but my ticket to the next destination was already prepaid and booked. I thought at the beginning of my planning the trip that it was smart to book in advance. I hoped I could concentrate on my journey instead of worrying about booking flights, but it left me with no control or say in the matter. The feeling that life was controlling me rather than my being the creator of my future reminded me of similar moments in the past decade. Once again, I had no choice but to roll with it.

Margarita Tartakovsky MS (*Are You Keeping Busy to Avoid Your Feelings?*, 2017) states that staying busy and finding activities to distract yourself is a common reaction to trauma. It's a method of survival because you don't allow yourself to feel; you just stay preoccupied and busy. So as painful as it may be, if you experience any kind of trauma or tragedy, I hope you give yourself the generous gift of time and kindness and allow yourself to feel. It's the only way to be strong and come out on the other side.

From Europe, I scheduled a group tour of Southeast Asia. I had never done any kind of tour and jumping into one that was a month long was probably not the best idea, but I decided to give it a go. I certainly didn't want to wander Asia, a land of limited English, by myself. The moment I went to my first group dinner, I wondered what

I'd gotten myself into. I chose the cheapest tour option and even that extended my budget to its maximum. I hadn't realized when I picked the "YOLO" tour that it would be mainly eighteen- and nineteen-year-olds. At thirty-one, I felt totally out of place. I tried to be friendly, thinking maybe we would connect, but with weeks of no sleep and 10 a.m. liquor shots happening on our bus daily, I felt annoyed. I thought about speaking up to my tour leader, asking if I could switch to another tour group, but talked myself out of it. I assumed the company already had exact numbers for the groups. As we packed up, traveled for hours, and unpacked, changing locations every few days, I realized I didn't like the nomad life. I really enjoyed staying in one place and feeling like a local there.

By the end of the Southeast Asian tour, I'd become friendly with two girls my age, but I was so over the constant travel, I just wanted it to stop. From there, I spent two weeks traveling solo in Bangkok and the Thai beaches, but really started to miss home and my friends, and I felt like I was in the middle of nowhere. The eleven-hour time difference made me feel alone with a million decisions to face. I continued on to Singapore, where I wandered aimlessly during the day with no plan other than to make the hours go by. At night, I used my tablet to call my friends and just cry to them. On my flight from Singapore to Bali, I reached a breaking point. As usual, we were given instructions to store our luggage and get ready for take-off. The flight attendant came by and informed me to buckle my seat belt. As soon as I did, I immediately unbuckled it and stood up.

"I need to get off!" I exclaimed.

The flight attendant assured me that once we landed in Bali, I'd be fine. We were taking off, and I couldn't deboard.

"I need to get off," I said again.

"Please, ma'am, take a seat."

With no choice, I sat down, and a young girl with beautiful, blonde hair who was sitting next to me asked, "Are you okay?"

Everything just poured out. I told her once we landed, I would arrive at the airport late at night and then have to take a cab ride solo to the town I had booked a hotel in three hours away. I mentioned that in the middle of the night, I couldn't stop crying and talking to my friends in the United States. She just sat and listened patiently.

Finally, about halfway through the short flight, she said, "I'm staying in a town not far from the airport, and it's just me. Would you like to stay for a few days? We could share the bed."

I know many people might think it was crazy both for a stranger to invite me over and then for me to accept. I truly felt I had no choice though, and after landing, I followed her to a driver who took us to the hotel.

Once I got there, all I wanted to do was sleep. She tried to invite me out each day, but I would just lie in bed staring at the ceiling, not being able to stop my constant thoughts. When she was out, I would try to call my friends during the day, but it was 1 a.m. where they were. I'd stay in the hotel room and try to keep busy, not sure what to do, but as each day passed, I knew I couldn't go any further. I found myself having really dark thoughts, and Christine and a few other friends would implore me to come home. I had the rest of my life to travel.

I Googled trips around the world and researched the people who went home early. Although we don't hear about it too often, it does happen. Traveling solo is a dream come true for many, but if the trip is not planned properly, and if traveling does not come naturally to you, it can end up being something negative you would've never expected. After reading the articles, feeling like I was just a shell of a person, and that my inside was already dead, I decided to go home. In a daze, I contacted the travel agency, and they said while I couldn't get any money back, I could use the rest of my tickets for a credit, which I could use to fly home.

I then packed up, said goodbye to my kind friend, and flew from Bali to Dubai. When I arrived in Dubai, all I kept imagining was lying in bed with my mom while she stood next to me petting my hair. At each leg of the journey, I kept repeating that I just needed to get home to her. In Dubai, I called her in a mass panic that I couldn't do it anymore. I couldn't move one more step. I couldn't handle one more flight. I would just stay in this airport the rest of my life. I was completely depleted of any energy or motivation to continue the journey ahead. I couldn't handle one more decision or moment surrounded by strangers. She commanded, "Sue, get on the plane. You aren't living there." I needed someone to tell me what to do. I obeyed, and after a very long flight and even longer trip, I finally saw her, and I was home.

Transformative Tip #14

Do you live with intention, or do you just exist? Every day I wake up, and I think about the purpose for my living that day. What do I want to accomplish? What kind of day do I want to have? Some may think this is silly. How can I control the type of day I have without knowing what type of obstacles may come my way? For me, though, it truly is magical. Throughout the day, if I'm not living up to the intention, I'm able to stop and pivot. For example, if my intention is to have a creative, productive day, and I notice at 1 p.m. I'm still sitting on the couch, I can remind myself I promised I would have a creative, productive day, and I can put plans in place to turn that day around. Anything that doesn't align with my mission is then dismissed. Sit around and do nothing? No! I said I would be productive. The promises we make to ourselves are often more powerful than the ones we make to others.

When I went on my trip, I had no intention of going halfway around the world. It was only to escape the panic I felt. If the trip was to explore what made me happy or experience different cultures, I would've made other choices than the one I did. If you find yourself making decisions that in your heart are not what you truly want, take it as a big sign you need to breathe, pause, and ask yourself, "Am I sure I want this?"

If you start to feel like a speeding train that won't stop, that life is happening *to* you not *for* you, then you must get someone else involved. Reach out and rise. Whether it be a friend, family member, or mental health professional, find someone who can support you.

CHAPTER 15: WHAT IS REALLY HAPPENING?

I, like many of you, thought the triumph part of the story would have begun by now. I thoroughly believed after making it home, things would've turned around. I was back in a familiar place surrounded by people who loved me. Unfortunately, I still didn't love myself. I spent the first few days sleeping all day and staying up all night. My ears would listen to the silence hoping to feel something. I was numb in every possible way: mentally, physically, and emotionally. I felt disconnected from everything and everyone. I existed solely because I knew if I waited long enough the sun would come up on the next day. I would pray if I could make it through this second, I could make it to a minute and then eventually an hour. I was listening to the clock tick, tick, tick. I would sleep in my mom's bed and listen to her breathe, inhaling and exhaling. As time went on, I'd feel frustrated I couldn't sleep and would get up and find our cat, Brownie. Though she usually didn't want to be held, she would let me pick her up and pet her for hours as I prayed to make it to the next day.

I'd eventually fall asleep for a few hours, waking up feeling just as tired as I did the night before. I'd try to talk to my mom, often feeling like my head would explode and that no matter how hard I tried, no one understood me. I had no hope for the future because I was too upset about my past. I was so confused about where I went wrong, feeling physically and mentally spent. I remembered my past South Beach life, and even though my friends were only an hour away, it felt like they were on the other side of the world. I couldn't think straight, and I couldn't sleep. I could only keep fighting to get through the day.

One day, I found myself on the kitchen floor, going back to being three years old, flailing my arms over something insignificant my mom said to me. My mom justified my temper tantrum by saying I was just overtired and continued on with her day. She said in time it would get better. I wondered if I stayed glued to Facebook, yearning for connection, even though I couldn't verbalize it. I would type just to be heard. The days turned into weeks, and I started to see darkness, and I felt like I was sinking into a pool where I couldn't swim. It just kept getting darker. It was like something had taken over my brain, and I just wanted the pain to go away. Brownie would continue to help me through the night. When I was in a fog, I would reach out to find her in the darkness of the house.

My mom didn't know what to do at this point. My brother kept saying I was too much drama for him. I felt like I couldn't breathe. My friends would continue to check on me, calling me on the phone and sending messages through Facebook, and I would put on my "everything is fine" face and tell them I would feel better soon. I really wasn't getting any better, though, I was slowly losing touch with reality. I barely knew what day it was.

My brain kept repeating, "End the pain, end the pain." I remember not being able to understand when I lost my brother and

Martha how someone could choose to end their life knowing how much it would hurt their friends and family. I kept thinking of them and how I had to do what my brother and Martha could not, I had to find a way out. I couldn't give up. I roamed around my mom's house looking at the old family pictures, thinking about how incomplete we had felt after half the people in the picture disappeared. I knew I couldn't put my family through losing another person unexpectedly. I kept repeating, "You can't pass your pain onto them, you can't pass your pain onto them." Yet, depression is a powerful force.

One day, my mom went out to do a few errands. After a few minutes, I felt an energy shift. I was all alone in this big house. I tried to breathe and talk to myself calmly, but my mind was raging, and it slowly accepted that life would be a lot better without my having to constantly fight the pain and heavy cloud surrounding me. Slowly, I dragged myself to my mom's room, feeling the heavy weight starting to separate from me. I was experiencing such mixed emotions. A war was being fought in my head and heart about what I *could* do, how I *could* take control back.

Suddenly, I heard a meow. I looked down and there was Brownie staring up at me with her big blue eyes. I smiled slightly, picked her up and brought her to the bed. She laid there and purred as I sat on Facebook interacting with friends again. I went to the bathroom and saw a container of bleach and had a fleeting thought, "What if I drank that? It could be that simple." I imagined pouring the bleach down my throat, but I couldn't actively reach for the bottle. In my gut, I knew I didn't really want to end my life.

I went back to petting Brownie and kept repeating, "Just keep petting the cat, just keep petting the cat, just keep petting the cat." I rapidly messaged a few friends. I had no idea what I was saying but later learned it didn't make much sense. Christine, Rachel, Sal, and a few other close friends connected with each other, and someone eventually called my mom. She told them I would be okay, but many of them had psychology and social work backgrounds, and they insisted she take me to a hospital.

She finally relented. The rest is a blur, but I remember a few moments. I recall getting in the car and there being an eerie silence. My mom is a chatterbox, so this was unreal. At the hospital as we waited in a room and I was lying in bed, it was like the floodgates opened. I told her everything I had kept in for so long. The rape, the toxic work environment, how the trip actually had gone, and I couldn't stop talking. The fight had gone out of me. I was just so scared. I had no concern for looking good or keeping her safe. It *all* came out. The doctor came in soon after and asked me a few questions.

Did I have thoughts of hurting myself, and did I have a plan? I answered yes to both questions. When you are that near death, your ability to lie greatly decreases, and you just want to stop the suffocating pain. After a few minutes, he told my mom they would need to admit me into the psych ward. I didn't resist because I knew I had no choice. My mom and I cried as she hugged me goodbye and told me she would be there the next day to see me.

I then had to strip naked to be examined before being given my hospital wear. It was like being stripped of my dignity because every mark on me was examined and analyzed. Finally, they had enough information and let me get dressed in a hospital gray shirt, pants, and socks. I thought that was bad, but it was about to get much more upsetting and scarier. As we walked through the locked doors with the loud clang behind me, I looked back and realized I was trapped. I was stuck there, and I couldn't leave! I heard the most frightening guttural screams as we passed by the patient rooms.

I was led to a room with a hard, bare metal bed. I was told lunch would be in an hour, and later in the day, I would meet with the doctor in charge. I wasn't hungry, so I asked if I could skip lunch, but they replied I had to report to lunch whether I was hungry or not. I was told at the moment I had no roommate, but that could change at any time. Then, I looked around and realized I was once again waiting for the minutes and hours to pass. I drove up the courage to go to the main living room area where people were spending time, and I sat down. A girl of about thirty years of age approached me, and I thought, "Okay, company."

The first thing she said to me with a blank stare was, "They are out to get me."

"Who?" I replied.

"The government—they are recording everything I do."

I gulped. I knew I had challenges, but this girl was completely in another world. I had no idea how to deal with her. Then someone ran screaming past me. I looked around, feeling my gut tighten up, and wondered how I ended up here. I searched for a place of calm, found a small nook with books, and breathed a sigh of relief. Books were always a symbol of something I could depend on. A way to escape any situation or circumstance. I took a book and sat down to read.

I learned to keep to myself, and keep my eyes on objects, not people. By lunch time I got in line, thinking this must be what jail is like. I got my foil covered apple juice and a sandwich. I quickly picked at the food and asked to go back to my room, but they said I had to wait for everyone else. I sat and listened to people talk and some of them actually sounded somewhat normal. I turned to speak with one girl, and she explained she was in the other wing for drug and alcohol abuse. She introduced me to a few people who, while struggling, seemed to at least be grounded in reality.

I was then sent to speak to the psychiatrist on duty in his office. I was relieved to have a few minutes of time with someone who was not a patient. We talked for a long time, and I told him everything. He said he would see me once a day until he felt I was ready to go home. He felt I had what was called "recurring depression" due to all the incidents that happened in my life. He said he would place me on some drugs to help me sleep and also to lift my mood. I would attend different therapy sessions from art, to music, to traditional group therapy to try to help improve my status. I just kept nodding, not taking in much of what he said.

I sat with the same group again at dinner. I learned more about their stories, and then we were all taken outside, which was really just a small block past the living room where people played catch. We were encouraged to exercise and be in the fresh air. We then were taken for "cocktails," which at first excited me, until I was given a white dixie cup of pills. I didn't fight it at all because I desperately wanted to feel better.

I called my mom and cried because she told me about my younger brother, and all the life happening outside the four walls of the hospital. I wanted to be with them, I wanted to be the old me, but she told me I needed to stay for my own good. I went back to my room, and there was a young girl on the other bed, my new roommate. She said she had been hospitalized before, and as neither of us could fall asleep, we lay awake talking. It felt better to feel less alone, to know I wasn't the only one feeling this lost. Eventually, we fell asleep just to be awakened by a loud commotion outside the door. A patient was hurling himself hard into his room door, and the hospital workers rushed in to help.

I just wanted out of the hospital, but I was stuck!

The next day my mom brought in a picture of my niece, who was now twelve years old. I put it on my dresser. Every time I thought about giving up, I'd think of her and how I needed to show her what strength was. She didn't deserve to lose another relative, and I thought about how accepted and adored I felt when I was with her. She gave me the strength for what I was about to do next.

The day started much like the day before, the same girl I met the first day approached me and said, "Hi, I'm Sara, and I'm being framed. The government is after you, too. You'll see if you use the phone, they will tap your calls."

Another person ran up to me and kept taking off their pants and putting them on, on and off, on and off. I knew I had to stand up and fight for myself. I knew being here wasn't helping. So, I went to my psychiatrist for my appointment as usual. He asked how things were going, and I told him about Sara and the guy removing his pants. I told him I was having a hard time, and he told me he would see what he could do.

About an hour later, a nurse knocked on my door, and said the doctor wanted to see me. When I approached the doctor's office, he told me to come in and sit down. He informed me he would be transferring me to the other wing. He said he saw that life had thrown me some curveballs, but I wasn't in as bad a mental state as many of the people there, and I really didn't belong in the mental illness wing. He shared that the drug and alcohol wing had an opening, and he would transfer me there. I was so relieved to know I was getting out. I grabbed my only possession, the school picture of my niece, and followed a nurse to the other wing, past the clanging alarmed doors.

As soon as I walked in, I felt better. There was a different, calmer, safer energy. A group was playing cards, and they invited me to join them. I wasn't as chatty as normal, but I gained confidence during the game and started to open up more. I thought maybe this wasn't so bad, but then I went to take a shower and realized there was no curtain bar, or curtain, and the door had no lock. I looked at my giant gray shirt and said, "This isn't me!"

I realized I wasn't there to stay, and I decided at that moment I was committing myself to living beyond those drab four walls. I wanted my life back, and I wanted to hug my friends. I wanted to go shopping with my niece. I wanted to experience another first kiss. I wanted to laugh with my mom.

That night, I prayed the following: "Dear G-d, I know we don't talk often anymore, and I know I am usually asking for something. Today I just wanted to say, if you help me get out of here, I promise I will *never, ever* get back here. I will do whatever you see necessary to make sure that doesn't happen. You name it, and I will do it. Please help me get out of here."

Two days later, my prayer was answered! The doctor said that while I wasn't fully recovered, he felt I could handle being home. He told me I would still be on medication for a while, and it was important that I took it daily. I also needed to find a therapist to continue to improve, but all I heard was "I'm going home!"

Something unexpected happened when they said my mom had arrived. I realized I would miss this place. I would miss not having to deal with a cell phone. I would miss the feeling of safety, and the routine the hospital had brought into my life. I would even miss some of the people—well maybe not the pants-less guy. I took a deep breath, grabbed my niece's picture, closed my eyes, thought of her, and stood up. I walked through the clanging alarm door for the last time. As I walked outside to my mom, I breathed the fresh air and took it all in.

Everything looked beautiful: the cars, the plants, even the hospital building. I was a bit scared to be on my own again without anyone there to help if I sunk too low, but I remembered my promise during the prayer, and I knew I would find a way to rise above my depression. Whatever it took, I would not be returning.

Transformative Tip #15

What stories do you tell yourself based on past experiences? Recognize what you're experiencing is influenced by a past lens. What often stops us from living our best life are the stories we tell ourselves. We don't look at what happened from an unbiased, unemotional viewpoint. We're looking through a lens influenced by our past pains and experiences. For example, a boss quickly passes you at work and doesn't even say hello, so you think she doesn't like you. Your brain links this experience to a memory of your mom quickly rushing into the house without acknowledging you. In that moment, you'd decided she didn't really love you. Now anytime someone hurries past, you assume they must not like you. Some things have nothing to do with us, yet we take them personally.

Practice asking yourself, "What is really happening? What are the facts, and what am I adding to the story to somehow feel better or justified?" We start off with a blank slate when we're born and then something happens to change that. Someone makes fun of us, we fail a test, or we ask someone out and get rejected. Suddenly, these circumstances have power over us. We live a little less and take fewer chances. Ask yourself, "What is the story behind this? What actually happened?" I look back on many of my traumas and can now see I was ruled by my emotions and blinded to what could be possible. Don't let your stories take away your power.

CHAPTER 16: ACCEPT WHAT IS

Go ahead. Take a deep breath and get a new box of tissues. You've been with me along this whole journey. You may have paused at certain points, but you always came back to read more! I know you've been anticipating this chapter for a long time. Congratulations! We have made it through some awful, challenging days together. I know your experiences may not have been the exact same, but I hope you can relate to parts of my story. Did you have days where your heart felt it was breaking in two? Perhaps days, you had to search for a reason to keep going?

So, you may be wondering, what happened next? What happens to someone when they become close to losing their life and actually get it back? Well, first of all, it wasn't instantaneous (yes, I can hear you groaning). The important part was with each small step, there was progress.

To start things off, my mom immediately drove me to therapy on a weekly basis. I met a few therapists but couldn't find the right fit for me. I felt they were more concerned with the time clock than my reasons for being there. Later, I learned that like any other doctor, you sometimes need to shop around. I did remember the doctor's orders and took my medications without a fight every single day.

I also emailed all my friends who I had kept so much from and told them everything. That in itself was really cleansing. I realized it was okay to take it easy. It was alright to slow down. It was acceptable to not always be the happy-go-lucky friend but to be honest and raw. As Ferris Bueller said, "Life moves pretty fast. If you don't stop and look around once in a while, you could miss it." This is a perfect quote for this particular situation!

Some of my friends called me and came up to visit. I was shocked to learn how many of them had therapists, or even parents with mental illness. Everyone had a story, and I felt completely accepted, not weird or judged in any way. I had no idea what was going to come next, and that was perfectly fine. I applied to a few local jobs, but my heart wasn't really into living in Florida anymore. I learned to enjoy the simple things with my family and realized how much I had taken them for granted. I was doing well and getting stronger. I yearned for my independence and some kind of direction. I would say to myself, "I survived the hospital, now what?"

Having a plan and a real ambition was important to me. I started to examine what my life was like in regard to my goals and standards instead of comparing myself to others. It was an odd feeling.

The best part of my day was engaging in phone calls with friends, which reminded me how many people cared and how there was still more life for me to experience. I was doing better, and my thirst for life increased, but I still felt I was ill equipped to go off on my own.

One night, my friend, Liz, called and told me she had just participated in a seminar, and wanted to know if I would join for her final session. I had no idea what the class was about, but the idea of seeing her face and receiving an invitation to something made me feel loved, so I immediately said yes. I remember how happy and excited she sounded, and I was glad to spend the time to see her. It felt *really* good that I could finally be there for a friend, completely present, while not having to make any sacrifices. The feeling of not having to leave for work mid conversation was awesome!

At the course conducted by Landmark Education, people shared their experiences, how life had shifted for them after only four days in the seminar. That open, vulnerable, authentic sharing spoke to my soul. I wasn't alone or an exception to the rule. I was normal! Many people there had experienced hard times of all different scales. Some didn't have any major traumas or tragedies but instead were there because they wanted lives full of empowerment and possibilities. No one's circumstances had changed in the four days, only their perspective of those circumstances and the power and ownership they were able to bring into their lives.

When the class ended, my friend shared with me that she was able to better handle work and realized that she could change jobs and possibly her career path. She asked me if I would be interested in registering for the seminar myself. Liz told me that because she had gained so much immediately, she knew she had to invite me. I had no money left having spent it all on my trip, but my fighting spirit was on fire! I finally saw a glimmer of hope, and the stories that the participants shared resonated with me deep inside.

I wanted that success story, the one told after the storm, the feeling that the future was all mine. I walked right up to the registration desk, took out my credit card, and signed up for the next course. I didn't know how I would pay for it, only that it wasn't merely something I wanted to do; it was something I needed to do. The part of me that had been silenced for so long was released. I deserved to have the best life possible. I would not give up, no matter the consequence.

I drove home that night smiling for the first time in a very long time. I had no idea what occurred, but something had transformed in me. I saw myself in the shared experiences. The support of the community and meeting a room full of people just like me had a true impact. They had been through struggles and allowed those situations to dictate who they were, limiting what was possible; but after the seminar, they had a new lease on life, a powerful way of being. I would never become that stuck, small person again. I came home that night with a smile on my face, kissed my mom on the cheek, and walked away, leaving her in shock.

A few weeks later, I participated in the same seminar. On the first day, the instructor wanted to make sure everyone was choosing to be there of their own volition and not by their desire to make someone else happy.

She asked, "Is there anyone who does not choose to participate in the rest of the course? We want to make sure you are powerfully choosing to be here. If you do not choose to continue, you may get all of your money back."

I felt my legs and arms rise. The reality of my having made a choice after being in victim mode and letting life just happen to me for so long hit me. I started to go toward the back of the room when she said, "Wait, stop, where are you going?" With a confused look on my face, I said "I'm leaving. I can't do this!"

She looked me straight in the eye and replied, "Yes, you can. Sit down."

Without a second thought, I found myself lowering into the chair and sitting up at attention. For someone to believe in me that much without even knowing me was inspiring. I had to stick around for more. By the first lunch break, people were approaching me saying how brave I was and that they also wanted to stand up but were too scared to admit they didn't think they were strong enough to stay. By dinner, I had a new group of friends, all out for the same purpose: to better themselves. At the end of the day, I had a flashback to college. I hugged everyone goodbye and drove home with cheeks that hurt from smiling for so long.

I was a different person by the last day of the course. I had laughed , cried, and transformed as only one can do in an environment where they care so much about other people's challenges. It's somehow healing. By practicing compassion for others, it's easier to practice it on ourselves. There's something magical when you work up the nerve to share your story with someone you've never met before. You really see that, as different as people are, we're all connected. Suddenly, your heart goes out to the woman who lost her son in an accident, and you realize that no matter what has happened in your life, you are still lucky compared to so many others.

On that final class day, my mom and my friend, Sarah, whom I invited to check out the course now that I was the one completing it, attended our final session. With them by my side, I stood up and shared my journey. I explained how I had been weighed down by my past, living as if my past were my present. I realized that I was not my past. I was not what had happened to me; I was not my past choices or circumstances. Instead, life was a wide-open place full of any possibilities I wanted to create. I shared that when the leader really saw who I was on the first day, it was like having someone clean off my glasses. I could finally look ahead. I could finally see what could be. I could make plans and create goals for my future and not only survive the day, but truly create anything I wanted for my future. The only thing that had been keeping me from the extraordinary life I wanted was believing in myself and giving up the idea that I needed to be perfect. Afterward, people came up to me and vulnerably shared the difference I had made in their lives over the course of that seminar.

While sharing in front of the room, I had announced that I was applying to jobs all over the United States that week. For many this may sound like no big deal, but it was such a sense of pride for me. I had spent years coming home from work, grabbing something to eat, and sitting down in front of my computer. As my mind would wander in the quiet of a late night, I would scroll the internet looking at jobs because I was unhappy. As I scrolled, my heart sunk over having to make a choice when I couldn't know how it would turn out. I talked myself out of applying. I may not have been happy at my job but at least it was predictable, in some ways I felt safe knowing what to expect from my boss or the guests. It may have not been enjoyable, but I feared what a new place or boss would be like. I dreamt about what it would feel like to not feel afraid and have faith that something new might actually be incredible! I needed to press that apply button. Then, my fingers froze, and I just couldn't do it. I would go to bed disappointed in myself. As often happens with abuse, I somehow had a fierce sense of loyalty and dependency on my boss and the company, even though I was being mistreated.

The fear of not being able to apply, or make any changes, was the same trepidation that kept me from speaking to my friend Martha about her shifts in behaviors. It was the same apprehension that kept me in Miami even though I would compare it to a black hole. Not having faith in yourself is one of the worst feelings. It's hard to want things and not be able to get them, always feeling they're at an arm's length. I had let my fear become so big and powerful that it tried to steal my life. In the seminar, I realized I had been treating imagined fears the same as if someone threatened me with a gun. I saw that my fear of not being good enough or being rejected was keeping me from what I most wanted in life. And I had allowed it to continue.

I was fed up. I didn't need to feel like the world was ending if I applied for a job and didn't get it or feel guilty for leaving a job that didn't work out for me. I was *not* a failure. My life was *not* over. I could create any kind of life I wanted. I was able to gain confidence and pride, and I knew no matter what I did or didn't do in life, it would all work out. Once we realize fear is the only thing holding us back, anything is possible. I asked myself, what is the worst that can happen? For example, I apply for a job and don't get it? So what? I can experience rejection and try to find another one. I decide to move to another city, but I don't like it? I can return back home.

A week after the seminar ended, I flew to Washington, D.C. for an in-person interview at a modern boutique hotel that was focused on empowerment and life-work balance. Two weeks after the seminar,

I hugged my mom goodbye and flew to the nation's capital to start a new life there. Yes! I had been offered the job. I truly felt trusted and valued. I spent two years in D.C. and was promoted twice.

I kept the promise I'd made that day while praying and went to the Washington, D.C., Department of Behavioral Health. They matched me with an amazing therapist, Elizabeth. She was unbelievable and truly changed my life. Our visits every week made me see how powerful the therapist-patient relationship could be. She realized that my job wasn't always easy. As I grew, I had to mature as a manager, and this came with pushback from my staff at times.

Elizabeth, through cognitive behavior therapy, made me feel proud of my growth. This therapy focuses on emotions and using your emotions as a tool rather than a weapon. I eventually came to understand not all emotions were bad and learned, when managed, they could actually help me to thrive. I took great pride in the ability to feel so much and care so much for others. The very first day, Elizabeth explained to me sometimes humans needed their brains rewired just like cars. I loved that analogy. There was nothing wrong with me that recreating my thought patterns couldn't change. When I realized I could control my brain instead of allowing it to control me, my entire being transformed. Every day after therapy, I'd walk down a big hill and stop at my favorite bakery to reward myself with a cupcake. It was nice to slow down, even just for five minutes. This cupcake symbolized the sweetness of life and of second chances.

I lived in D.C. for those two years, became an assistant organizer of a wine lovers' meet-up, and met people from all around the world. I learned to appreciate not having a car and not having to deal with traffic or parking. I even chose to live in one of those high rise buildings, the type I had coveted for so long. This one even had a large pool and view of Rock Creek Park. Living in a place where so much change had occurred for so many different types of people truly inspired me. I would visit the monuments and the National Mall and take in the strength of this nation and the courageous people who hadn't allowed themselves to be stopped by their circumstances. My favorite was Abe Lincoln's memorial. I used to call him my boyfriend because we'd spend evenings together watching the sunset looking out on the reflecting pool where I paused and processed on how far I'd come. My new manager would tell me to sleep in on days that were lower occupancy. She truly invested in me.

I will never forget one of my bosses, John, who said to me one day during a one-on-one conversation, "Get up and take my seat. I know you want to better learn payroll. Now you are the driver. I will sit next to you and navigate."

I was only at the job for six months, and being given the keys to more responsibility brought my happiness to a whole new level. After many years, someone took the time to teach me about the financials, the area I had always wanted to learn but never had anyone invest their time to teach me. Within my first year, the middle of 2015, I was promoted to another hotel in the company.

At the next hotel, we were taking over a property that was changing companies and introducing them to our brand. The old staff there didn't love that their managers had been fired and we were brought on instead. I had to put all my focus into my sessions with Elizabeth because some strong, stubborn staff members were testing my emotional progress. One girl, Suzy, would adamantly refuse to listen to me, and we often argued. Eventually she went to Human Resources and got my boss involved. The general manager, Thomas, later spoke to me, and I became determined to own the tone and words I chose when I spoke to people. I realized the importance of creating relationships with my staff and earning their respect before telling them what to do. With the advice of my manager Rachel, I took Suzy out to Starbucks, a neutral territory, to get to know her and start over. I had spent so much time feeling I needed to protect myself at work that I had grown to take most reactions personally. After talking to Suzy, I learned about her family and realized she was only tough because she had to be. I began to understand that, from her perspective, one day her managers were gone, and there I was telling her what to do. I realized everyone has a story, a reason they are the way they are. A strong manager knows how to connect on a human level first and a boss/employee level second. I decided to find a way for my work relationships to be a testing ground for standing up for myself in a way that the other person receives the message. I learned that, if I were vulnerable and let my guard down, the other person would often do the same.

Elizabeth supported me in many ways as I grew in my relationship building and communication. I'd see her after work and we'd discuss the emotions that came up for me and how to better manage them. One day I saw one of my staff, Becca, crying on the steps. We began a conversation, and she reminded me of myself in so many ways. She was trying so hard to balance what was going on in her personal life with dedicating herself to our guests each day with a positive attitude. That day, she saw me as more than a boss. She saw me as a person, and I saw the difference I could make for people by sharing some of my story. We connected on a whole other level, and my pride and strength only became stronger.

By April 2016, I didn't need to ask my boss if I was doing a good job or not. Our increased staff and guest satisfaction scores and the feeling of fulfillment I felt everyday spoke volumes. I had learned to appreciate the small steps that lead us to bigger goals. I communicated to myself how I would speak to a close friend, acknowledging myself for what I had accomplished each day rather than focusing on the mistakes I'd made. Biggest of all, I embraced the idea that on some days, I had accomplished enough. If the next shift was busy, it was fine to go home. I was enough, and I had done my part. Often, the best gifts are the ones you give yourself. For me, the gifts of self-grace and appreciation showed to be invaluable.

I decided to apply for my boss's job because she was leaving. The general manager, Thomas, was straightforward in his communication during my interview. Although I had greatly grown, he didn't consider me for the role due to that incident with Suzy in the beginning of the year. What I was surprised by most was what came next. I walked out of the room, deep in thought. I felt my gut speaking to me. I no longer was ruled by my initial emotional responses. Instead, I embraced the value of a pause and a breath. I took a moment to think about what had happened and what my options could be in responding to the situation. It was a gift to be able to feel and to experience my emotions. Emotions were not bad, scary, or uncontrollable. I no longer let circumstances or other people's decisions or opinions impact my day. My feelings about my self-worth did not come from needing to be approved by another person. I would not be held back by my general manager.

That night, with a clear, focused head, I immediately logged online and viewed all the other front office manager jobs in the company. Within a week, I had an interview at a hotel in Boston. Three weeks later, I was packing again—this time to be the head of the Front Office department. This was something I'd dreamed about ever since my first day as a front desk agent.

Upon leaving, Suzy gave me a big hug, told me how much I meant to her, and how sorry she was for giving me a hard time at first. As I took off on my flight to Boston, I looked down at all the monuments and the city I had come to love and knew I could handle whatever came next.

In Boston, I felt like a celebrity. As soon as I checked into my hotel room, I saw a personalized card welcoming me, a huge fruit plate, and lots of other goodies. There was also a white pillow embroidered with "Wicked Smaht," which made me laugh. I was able to easily walk from the hotel around the city and loved the smell of water and the sight of seagulls again. I walked to the market and saw aisles and aisles of seafood. I decided this could work! I quickly focused on getting to know my team and found a beautiful modern apartment in a great building only one train stop from work.

By the end of the year, I had accomplished and experienced my goal of heading up a department. I then realized something important. While I loved managing my team and having such an impact on the hotel and its guests, I didn't like some of the other managers who only wanted to do things as they'd always been done. My new ideas were shot down with "that's not how we do it here." My team of only nine people meant I often had to stay late and cancel my dates and other plans if anyone happened to call out of their shift.

My boss, Harald, was amazing. He would cover for me, so I could see my therapist at the same day and time each week. He also tried to give me a day off after working overnight shifts. After a while, I started to want more than just the title and knowledge of being a top dog. I wanted a balanced life. Every time I saw my niece and sister or visited my NYC friends, I wondered why I was so close yet so far away. I wanted to be able to celebrate happy hours and see them every weekend. I pined for my weekends to be spent not working! I was tired of my life being defined by work.

When I went to sign my lease, my gut again spoke to me. It said, "You don't really want to do this." I felt like Boston had nothing left to show me, and it was time to go home. It was time to go back to New York where it all began. One of my biggest regrets was that I hadn't lived in the same city as my niece since she was one year old. My college friends had gotten married and had kids, and I wanted to get to know them, too. I quit my job in August of 2017 and moved to Queens without a job or perfect plan in sight. My friend Carla scouted an apartment for me on Craigslist, and my landlord mailed me the keys.

As I got off the bus, I looked up as I always did when I arrived in New York City and saw the Empire State Building while walking toward the subway. It was a symbol of how I now saw myself: strong, full of hope, consistent, and powerful. I dragged my suitcase to the subway and sitting on the train in midsummer filled me with calm and happiness. People from all ages and walks of life were smiling and laughing together. It felt like a utopia, and no one knew my past, only me. I knew how much I'd survived, learned, and experienced. I was part of something bigger than myself; I was part of the community of New York!

Upon exiting the train, I saw the Sunnyside Arch welcome sign and smiled to myself. When I found out my building was called "The Bliss," I almost cried. I pressed the elevator button and thought back as I went up to the sixth floor. I was no longer in my first-floor apartment in Miami, where people would knock on the window to be let in at all hours of the night. I was now on the top floor. This symbolism was not lost on me. I found my apartment, slowly pushed the door open, and walked into the rest of my life. Full of light and love, adventure and triumph, I would finally reach the sky.

Transformative Tip #16:

How often do you resist parts of your life? How often do you resist accepting how someone is and expect them to change? Accept what is instead of resisting. As humans, we have this need to be in control and in charge. We wake up in the morning, get ready for work, and come upon a car accident or train delay. We get upset, frustrated, and mad. We can't control it, so why let it get to us? The longer we react, the more it will impact the rest of our day. Instead, we can just accept that there was a car accident and put a good song on Spotify or use the time to read our favorite book on the train. What you resist persists. My resistance to my assault had a huge impact on my life. Rather than just accepting I was assaulted, I judged myself for putting myself in that situation. I denied something like that could happen to me. Whatever you're most unhappy with in your life, either accept it or take action to change it. After all, action moves our lives.

The most important action one can take is reaching out for help. This can take a huge amount of courage and be a scary experience. If you don't reach out, though, you'll continue to feel the same way. We can easily predict our future by looking at our current habits and routines. Is this the life you want to keep living? If the answer is no, realize you deserve to be supported. We are not meant to get through life alone. Allowing other people to contribute to you is one of the greatest gifts we can give each other. Even if you think you're a bother or a burden, I promise at least one person wants to try to help you be happy again.

EPILOGUE: LEARNING HOW TO FLY

So how exactly did I go from surviving to thriving? Throughout the book, I've shared with you some of the lessons I picked up along the way. There's always more to learn and explore, though. First of all, the greatest lesson I learned was that my depression will never be magically cured. Trauma and tragedy can be reframed, or seen in a different perspective, but they always have to be managed. This is why many therapists have their own therapists. They know life is a journey, full of many experiences and major growth. It is impossible to be happy all the time, and it's acceptable to have a bad day. It's okay to struggle. What's not workable is when you start to feel you're a victim of that bad day and stop taking action.

Being aware of yourself, of when you stop acting or feeling like yourself, is very important. As a survival mechanism, our minds and bodies often want to escape pain when it becomes too difficult. It's easy to numb with alcohol, sex, keeping busy, not being fully present, or avoiding things that make you feel alive. What's even worse, is this can happen without us even realizing that all we're doing is trying to escape reality. Reality, as much as we try to run and avoid it, is still there tomorrow. Being brave enough to admit that something doesn't leave you feeling at peace is vital to your not being destroyed by pain.

Numbing is a temporary Band-Aid. It helps you survive but certainly not thrive.

So, if you begin to feel numb or disconnected, what can you do? You can take action, no matter how small. Wake up and think of one thing you can do today. Maybe it's sharing with a friend you're having a bad day, maybe it's going for a run, or maybe it's journaling. Celebrate each small action you take. Action makes the world go around. It gets us what we want most in life. Thoughts are nice, dreams are helpful, but action—that's where it's at.

The notion of *I've worked on my mind enough, I'm done*, doesn't exist. Do you say to yourself, "Okay, my body is fine, so I'm never exercising again?" No! Things fall apart when you think you're finished and take your foot off the gas. It's suddenly hard to walk up a set of subway stairs, you feel less energized, or you start to gain weight. It's the same with your mind. Tony Robbins (*Why growth is a never-ending journey*, 2016) says it best: "If you're not growing, you're dying." Our minds and emotional fortitude are not meant to be neglected. If we're open, we can constantly experience breakthroughs that can shift our lives and open up possibilities for us to grow and understand. We're all works in progress, and once you accept the point of life is the journey, you can transform into someone you hardly recognize. That's how amazing you are.

I'm always on this quest for transformation and growth. There is no cookie cutter answer. You need to do what works for you, whether it's formal therapy in an office, group therapy, music therapy, art therapy, or an online support group. It could also be a nontraditional approach such as reiki, meditation, or hypnotism. You could seek personal development by choosing to join programs such as Landmark Education or attend one of Tony Robbins' events. What matters is that you release your spiritual side and support your soul to reach its full potential.

So how can you begin to thrive today? Below are some ways I've already shared with you.

1. Accept you are constantly growing. Question who you are and who you've been led to believe you are.
2. Be curiously engaged. Use as many of your senses as possible.
3. Self-celebrate! Increase your awareness of how you speak to yourself.
4. Plan action steps and deadlines, and realize failure is to be expected and embraced.
5. No decision is permanent.
6. Limit your time on social media, especially if you find yourself comparing your life to others.
7. The only person you need to make happy is yourself.
8. Pause and invest in yourself.
9. Emotions are there to be experienced. As painful and intense as they can be, feel it to heal it.
10. Acknowledge others for what they do.
11. Be in the moment.
12. Practice gratitude.
13. Listen to your gut.
14. Understand the only one responsible for your life is you.
15. Live with intention.
16. Recognize your triggers and stories.

17. Accept what *is* instead of resisting it.
18. Ask for help when needed.

I want to make sure you receive value from this book, so here are a few bonus suggestions:

Remember to celebrate. Every. Day. I would have week-long celebrations for my birthday for over a decade because it was a huge deal to me. Now I see it was because, most days, I didn't feel very special. I didn't feel like I mattered or was worth celebrating. This is why I tried to cram all of my happiness into one week and would wish I had the time off to enjoy the people in my life more. Now I celebrate every day and focus on self-care, on choosing a job that allows me to have a strong work-life balance every single day, so my cup can be full and running over. It takes some work to be in the moment, but it's definitely worth it to feel alive.

The brain is a very powerful organ. What we focus on is what begins to appear in our lives. For example, I was thinking about how many of my friends were getting pregnant, and I suddenly saw pregnant women and kids everywhere. This part of the brain is called the reticular activating system, it filters out what you have deemed as unnecessary, so the important information goes through. I was thinking so much about my friends and pregnancy all I could see was pregnant women everywhere. Has something like that ever happened to you? If you focus on an affirmation such as I am powerful and today will be a good day, you start to notice the good moments of that day.

Always remember you control your brain; it does not control you. Due to social media, information is always at our fingertips. You get to choose if this tool will empower, connect, and support you or create isolation, exhaustion, and a feeling of not being good enough. Recently, I noticed a lot of negative postings on my Facebook feed. I would feel down and empty the more I looked. I wanted to find a way to change my main influences from negative to positive. I wanted to change who I was surrounded by, so I started enrolling in personal development seminars and made some like-minded friends.

Currently my page is flooded with positive and supportive postings. I learned that *you* control and create the social media world you participate in. I learned that *you* control the actions you take and what you use the internet for. I learned *you* control connecting virtually rather than with a phone call or in person. I learned *you* are in the driver's seat.

Most importantly, remember you are not your past. For too long, I would mentally read over my stories and pour all of my energy into wanting to go back and fix or change those past experiences. Imagine constantly rethinking high school and wanting to go back and do it again. You would be missing out on your life today.

The moment I chose to step out of the darkness and into the light, to not bury my past but to make peace with those experiences and release them, was the moment I was "reborn." That was the instant I realized I had to write this book. Deciding to make the choice to do whatever it takes to have a better life without knowing how it would happen was the moment I became alive. How often do you become obsessed with how you're going to do something rather than just deciding what you want and figuring out how to achieve it later? Too often we focus on what we don't have or what we haven't accomplished. Focus on what already fulfills you, and channel that energy into spending your days doing whatever that is or surrounding yourself with whoever that is.

I want you to have the most amazing, extraordinary life possible, no matter how long it takes. Don't give up; your story is not done yet. We are all on a journey. Give yourself some grace. We're not wooden statues; we're more like clay. Who will you mold yourself to be? It all starts with a little self-love, acceptance, kindness, and a deep breath.

I will leave you with one final thought. Your voice is possibly the most powerful, richest possession you will ever have. Use it! We all have a story, one that can help to heal someone else. It's easy to think you're alone, that no one understands your journey, or that your story isn't worth telling. By reaching out, by sharing, you can truly rise and realize how much you matter.

Never let anyone make you feel that you should swallow what's inside your heart, or what is on the tip of your tongue. If we don't share our experiences, they will become trapped inside. Self-expression is one of the best gifts we've been given. My life changed forever when I realized we have the power to change the way we see what's happened to us.

Recognize if you're just getting through the day or if you're taking actions to get you closer to truly living. Your past will be your past, but your future... well, that's up to you. You choose what to focus on. Check in with yourself daily, and truly allow yourself to feel—all of it! Feel everything because it means you're alive. The next time you're struggling, remember every struggle is an opportunity to learn and grow. Please give yourself a gift, and take those painful, hard days and turn them into something wonderful.

"Sometimes in tragedy, we find our life's purpose." — Robert Breault

THE END.

SOURCES

Are You Keeping Busy to Avoid Your Feelings? (2017, July 12). Psych Central. https://psychcentral.com/blog/are-you-keeping-busy-to-avoid-your-feelings

Best Robert Brault Quotes | The Cite Site Quatations Page. (n.d.). The Cite Site. https://thecitesite.com/authors/robert-brault/

Clarkson, K. (2004, November 30). *Breakaway [Breakaway]*. RCA records.

Grateful vs thankful: Choose wisely to boost your happiness and success. Smart Leadership Hut. (2017, August 2018) https://smartleadershiphut.com/motivation/grateful-vs-thankful/

How to Power Through Your Quarter-Life Crisis. (n.d.). The Muse. https://www.themuse.com/advice/powering-through-your-quarterlife-crisis

Inspiringquotes.us. (n.d.). *Top 30 quotes of POPE PAUL VI famous quotes and sayings | inspringquotes.us.* Inspiring Quotes. https://www.inspiringquotes.us/author/6535-pope-paul-vi

Menken, A, & Ashman, H. (1991, November 22). Belle [Beauty and the Beast]. Walt Disney.

Millennials struggle with "quarter-life crisis." (2018, March 20). Washington Examiner. https://www.washingtonexaminer.com/red-alert-politics/millennials-struggle-with-quarter-life-crisis

19 Signs You're Experiencing a Quarter Life Crisis (+ Test). (2020, November 13). LonerWolf. https://lonerwolf.com/quarter-life-crisis/.

Nothing is as painful as staying stuck - Narayana Murthy. (2021, January 28). Inspire99. https://inspire99.com/nothing-is-as-painful-as-staying-stuck-where-you-dont-belong/.

120 Brilliant Theodore Roosevelt Quotes on Leadership and Life. (2019, January 18). Planet of Success. http://www.planetofsuccess.com/blog/2019/theodore-roosevelt-quotes/

Pitbill, & Christina, A. (2012, November 16). *Feel This Moment* [Global Warming]. Mr 305, Polo Grounds, RCA Records.

"Pope Paul VI quotes and sayings," July 12, 2017 https://www.inspiringquotes.us/author/6535-pope-paul-vithe musepo.

Smith, W. (1998, July 20). Just the Two of Us [Big Willie Style]. Colombia.

Smith, W. (1998, November 23). *Miami* [Big Willie Style]. Sony

Tips for Talking with Survivors of Sexual Assault | RAINN. (2019). Rainn.org. https://www.rainn.org/articles/tips-talking-survivors-sexual-assault

Toxic positivity: Definition, risks, how to avoid, and more. (2021, March 31). Www.medicalnewstoday.com. https://www.medicalnewstoday.com/articles/toxic-positivity

Why growth is a never-ending journey. (2016, August 29). Tonyrobbins.com. https://www.tonyrobbins.com/mind-meaning/why-is-growth-addictive/

Printed in Great Britain
by Amazon

70937934R00119